Friends in a Hundred Places

Friends in a Hundred Places

✦

43 YEARS OF TRAVELING THE BACK ROADS OF THE US AND CANADA

William F. Mason

iUniverse, Inc.
New York Lincoln Shanghai

Friends in a Hundred Places
43 YEARS OF TRAVELING THE BACK ROADS OF THE US AND CANADA

iUniverse books may be ordered through booksellers or by contacting:

iUniverse
2021 Pine Lake Road, Suite 100
Lincoln, NE 68512
www.iuniverse.com
1-800-Authors (1-800-288-4677)

ISBN-13: 978-0-595-38622-2 (pbk)
ISBN-13: 978-0-595-83002-2 (ebk)
ISBN-10: 0-595-38622-9 (pbk)
ISBN-10: 0-595-83002-1 (ebk)

Printed in the United States of America

Dedicated to my beloved wife, Marilyn

Contents

INTRODUCTION

I've been a motorcycle rider for over 60 years, beginning as a commuter in the crowded areas around New York City, progressing to week-end trips and organized motorcycle activities, and in recent years to extended trips around the country. In the middle years my son and I bought, repaired, and sold motorcycles and traveled together on week-long trips into the country. On these longer trips we began to realize that the motorcycles themselves were a sufficient attraction to facilitate meeting new people. Talking with them was almost as enjoyable as riding the machines and passing through new places. In fact, for me the enjoyment of developing friendships and experiencing life in places that are markedly different from where I have lived became a major objective in my travel plans.

People are remarkably curious when they come across a motorcycle from another state, especially if it is loaded with camping luggage. This curiosity has been a major factor in my development of conversations with hundreds of people and the majority of "adventures" listed in the table of contents of this book. One distinctive characteristic of my travels is the personal involvement I have established with people in the places I've visited.

The practicalities of working for a living and raising a family tend to limit the places most motorcycle enthusiasts can get to on their machines. Most bikers are limited to local travel, and possibly an annual trip to one of the big regional motorcycle rallies. On these occasions they share stories about their riding experiences. This book is like a collection of such stories, any one of which a rider might consider to be the most memorable he or she ever experienced. It relates my experiences on annual "tours" for over 40 years, covering, very roughly, 50,000 miles of American and Canadian roads.

The rapidly growing numbers of couples that are beginning to tour by motorcycle are beginning to develop a spirit of friendship with each other, but they seldom take time to develop a dialog with other people in the areas they pass through With their matching clothes and helmets—connected by wire with music, CB radio and cell phone features, they ride in comfort, generally on the main roads, and often pulling motorcycle trailers full of even more comforting stuff. I meet them in campgrounds or in motels and enjoy swapping stories about our travels. (The comfort they have that I envy most is the female companionship.) But heir emphasis on comfort, security and their families buffers them from the kind of experiences you will read about here. We will meet some of them.

The fascinating events described in this book have taken place on long motorcycle trips from my home in Virginia, while touring twenty four of the eastern United States and seven of the ten Canadian Provinces. In March of each year I begin to anticipate the spring and summer and riding through the country, tent camping and entering the world of small towns and new experiences. The anticipation of these trips initiates an almost pathological change of mood that continues to develop even as I'm leaving on a trip. This book describes that mood and recounts the many different aspects of my riding experiences.

In my view, the best way to enjoy the full pleasure of motorcycle riding is to journey for at least a week alone—enough time to awaken some of the sensors that most of us seldom stimulate in our everyday routines and enough freedom from schedules to explore whatever comes to mind. The experience is strangely similar to the effects of meditation. From what I read about meditation, it involves a sort of relaxed concentration that moves primary brain activity from the more action-oriented right side to the calmer, less frantic left side and increases the sensitivity of all the body's sensors. A few hours motorcycling alone on the road has a similar effect. Has this anything to do with the "Freedom" thing? I think so.

Every motorcyclist seems to have his or her own special interpretation of what is called, in over-simplified terms, "freedom." No doubt you have seen Harley Davidson advertisements for their "Freedom Machines." I'm kind of cool on their use of the term because to me it implies that, when a rider jumps on a motorcycle, he or she feels that they are leaving most of the rules that define generally "acceptable" social behavior. Harley's current ads point out quite correctly that a motorcycle "can truly transport you into a different state of mind"[1]...for those who enjoy "a philosophy of living where the only boundaries are the pavement and how far you're willing to go."

---

1.   Harley Davidson advertisement in *Motor Trend* dtd March 2006

For me the Freedom thing is the "different state of mind" that comes with the escape that people experience as they move vicariously into movies or books, and drop all consideration of schedules, appointments and rituals and patterns of thought and behavior that are part of what is generally considered their "normal" life—but it is not freedom from established rules of behavior.

As I roll out into the countryside on my motorcycle, I feel that I'm leaving a state of mind. Part of it is that I'm "going into the scene!" to use Persig's phrase from *Zen and the Art of Motorcycling.*[2] I am no longer seeing the world pass by my windows…I'm entering into the world of fresh unprocessed air. I am joining nature, sensing its smells and sounds, its sunshine and rain, all of which are normally buffered out of our daily working lives. No longer just an observer, the rider is now part of the scene.

It takes a couple of days for my definition of the "freedom" feeling to be recognized and to see how it influences life "on the road." Here is how it evolves. A few miles down the road, after leaving thoughts about adequate preparations for the trip, my mind begins to reorient the ordinary thought patterns of my daily life, primarily the organizing of each day's anticipated activities, schedules and commitments, each with its own alternatives and impacts, the kind of things we think about on our way to our jobs. A few more miles and my mind has displaced these patterns as it responds to the immediate and changing stimulation from the awakening physical senses; the "feel" and sound of the machine and the road, the fresh air and unfamiliar sounds and scenery—somewhat like the experience of a movie-goer or book reader when he or she enters the book or movie world.

As this displacement phenomenon continues I sometimes morph into what you might say is another persona, one that is possibly more "complete" in that I'm dealing with inputs from all my body's senses rather than just the ones used to deal with my "normal" societal environment.

Perhaps this "transition" metamorphosis partially explains the motivation of many kinds of out-of-doors oriented sea, mountain and wilderness adventurers who enjoy being separated from their regular routines. In my case, the influence of a lifelong love of engines, especially those that have aesthetic appeal, as is the case with modern motorcycle engines, adds to the sense of pleasure that comes from the changed circumstances.

Someone has said that a wise man travels to discover himself. Although it's not clear to me what this really means, it may refer to this change in awareness that a motorcycle rider develops as he adjusts to the riding experience. A traveler, tem-

---

2.   Pirzig,Robert M…*Zen and the Art of Motorcycle Maintenance.* Bantom Books, Inc.

porarily uncoupled from his or her regular surroundings has some time and sufficient isolation to let his or her mind roam. Traveling by motorcycle generates an interesting vigor in the mind. Separated from having to deal with its usual considerations, the mind still seems to have a need to keep busy, as evidenced by the popularity of books, movies, television, card games, and crossword puzzles. As it sheds its regular agenda, it seeks new things to think about. Samuel Johnson observed that, "The mind is never satisfied…and is always breaking away from the present moment and losing itself in schemes of future felicity…."[3].happiness, that is. Time can be spent on fantasies. Things that stimulate curiosity are allowed to take some time, i.e. the rider is free to investigate whatever comes to mind or comes his way, (except, of course, when he's hungry). This generally leads to new experiences and, after all, as someone has noted, "Experience is what you have left when everything else is gone."

And, now at age 81, the author would add that appreciation of one's experiences grows with age. As this story unfolds, there will be ample evidence of my pleasure in remembering mine and lots of illustrations of how the above thoughts and ideas have influenced my life with my motorcycle.

---

3.   Johnson, Samuel. *The Rambler*, Personal Paper No. 2, March 24, 1750,

1

THE MOTORCYCLIST'S DREAM TRIP

THE BASIC PATTERN OF MY TRIPS

As mentioned earlier, I had ridden motorcycles for several years before I began taking long distance touring trips some forty-plus years ago in 1960.

There are a few aspects that all the trips have in common. The weather is the main cause of variations from them.

In July and August, when I make most of my trips, I usually wear bright colored clothing so I can be more easily seen. If it's raining, I wear old sneakers rather than boots or regular shoes covered by totes. In colder months, I, of course, wear a jacket and a scarf.

Weather permitting; I sleep in my tent about half the nights, preferably close to very small towns where I can enjoy company in a local bar. I enjoy the tent from the minute when I climb into it at night, laying there reviewing the day and floating in a variety of fantasies. And I enjoy the occasional morning when I'm still in my sleeping bag when the sun brightens the canvas and I'm trying to remember exactly where I am.

When it's convenient to use an established campground for tenting, I often make friends through the children. While I assemble the tent, some will come to look at the motorcycle. Father occasionally follows. If no kids come over, I go to the nearest neighbor to borrow something people don't mind lending—like a hammer or hatchet to help put in my tent stakes. Conversation about the motorcycle or my travels usually develops, especially if I'm out of Virginia, Usually, I get invited to an evening campfire, and again, for a cup of coffee as I'm packing up in the morning.

I carry no cookware or food. When tenting, I rise early to swim or shower if one is available, break camp and ride an hour or so before seeking a big breakfast, my favorite meal.

After a night in my tent, I often have to pack it up wet from rain or morning dew. By the time I stop for breakfast, the sun is usually up and while I have breakfast I spread the tent over the motorcycle to (partially) dry it.

If it isn't raining, I take a daily swim in a river or a lake. To find swimming places, I choose roads along streams or rivers and often stop and talk to young people along the roads or in small towns. Sometimes I just cool off in a river. I choose motels with pools. Later we'll talk about locating swimming holes using the Internet.

I wash my socks, T-shirts and underwear in swimming holes, hotel sinks or in showers at campgrounds.

I've found myself a lot more comfortable and my conversations a lot less stunted, when I represent myself as an electrician, rather than trying to explain or answer questions about my life and career in the suit-and-tie world, the complex and "un-natural" world of electronic technology and government contracting. We'll see how this works later.

I dream up fuzzy plans for each day while still in the bedroll and usually change them a few times, starting right after breakfast.

I call my wife when I settle on a place for the night, or when I need her help to find a motel using the web. On the last couple of trips I've had a cell phone.

A BRIEF LOOK AT WHERE I LIVE

I am fortunate that the roads in any direction from my home on a lake near Fredericksburg, Virginia, are great for motorcycling. All around us are reminders of colonial history, the American Revolution, and the Civil War. We're close to the great homes and estates of Washington, Jefferson, Madison, Monroe, Lee, Jackson, John Marshal, and Woodrow Wilson. Farms, rivers and "horse country" connect us to the ocean on the east or to the beautiful Blue Ridge Mountains to the west. As I leave on my annual trips along the nearby roads on a sunny morning, I see cows and horses look up—smile, or sometimes grumble amongst themselves as if speculating on "wonder where he's headed this time..." Here and there I get a smile and a wave from someone at their mailbox, or drinking coffee on their porch. The hum of the motorcycle engine seems to stimulate a friendly reaction that makes me feel I could stop anywhere and make a new friend.

When I head south, the first time my feet get off the bike's foot pegs is usually at a coffee shop near the serpentine brick walls of the magnificent University of Virginia campus that Jefferson designed in Charlottesville. For me, this campus is as great a memorial to him as the Jefferson memorial is in Washington. The monument records some of his greatest words, but the University in Charlottesville and his home at Monticello reflect his life.

A short distance west of home, I can look down from the Blue Ridge Mountain's Skyline Drive on a spectacular panorama of peaceful farms and little towns in the Shenandoah Valley. Being a Civil War buff, the valley stimulates my memory of the legendary Stonewall Jackson's small but quick moving "foot cavalry" of less than 17,000 men defeating three Federal armies totaling over 60,000 troops sent by Lincoln to destroy him. I can imagine his dedicated troops moving so quickly that the people of Washington suspected that there must be more than one Jackson—and that the great one might enter Washington at any time.

To the southeast I've enjoyed Virginia's Colonial History with trips to Jamestown, Williamsburg and Richmond. Further east of home is the Atlantic Ocean, my gateway to trips both north and south along the Atlantic shore. North is Washington, Baltimore, Philadelphia and N.Y. City, all of which I enjoyed in the early years of riding when I sought places to visit. Only later did I develop the strong desire to enjoy life on the road more than the places the roads took me to. I try to avoid the congestion of these cities now, and usually circle west around them to New England and the Maritimes.

My local riding has uncovered a great variety of interesting places. Famous battles of the Civil War took place a few miles from my home; Battles in the Wilderness, Chancellorsville, Manassas, Kelly's Ford and Brandy Station are recorded on many miles of National Park Service historical signs around the area. But visiting by motorcycle allows me to develop a more personal appreciation of the places than a typical tourist gets. This will be seen throughout this book, but let me give an early example.

A few years ago I passed a road sign labeled "Madden's Tavern" for a side road about half-way between Fredericksburg and Culpeper. It was a dirt road then (now paved) but I wondered if it related to the popular John Madden of football fame, so I turned my motorcycle into the road to investigate.

About two miles in, I came upon an old house with a battered old sign hanging on the driveway that said "Maddens Tavern." Recognizing that it was very old and located in the middle of where many famous civil war actions had occurred, especially Brandy Station, and Kellys Ford, I looked for someone to ask about the tavern.

Finding none I rode over to the area's primitive post-office-in-a-trailer (in Lignum) and asked if the postmaster there knew anything about its history. He told me that Mr. Madden was very friendly and often chatted with the mail delivery lady.

I visited with Mr. Madden several times on week-end rides and we became good friends. He enjoyed talking to me about my motorcycle travels and telling me fascinating stories about things that happened when the tavern had served both the Confederates and the Yankees as the region "changed hands" several times during the Civil War.

Mr. Madden (T.O. Madden—*my first "new friend"*) was the great-great-grandson of an Irish indentured servant, Sarah Madden. Sarah was indentured in 1759 to pay her pauper debts—as a house servant to President Madison's father in his mansion named Montpelier. In his will, Madison gave Sarah papers showing that she was a "free" person. Sarah then left the Madison family and went to work as a seamstress and washerwoman in nearby Culpeper and with her half-black son eventually bought the land where she and her son opened "Madden's Tavern. The tavern prospered, serving both the north and the south in the civil war as the battle lines changed around the Madden property many times.

In the early 1800s the Tavern was a resting place for overnight travelers, mostly drovers and teamsters, traveling the thirty odd miles of dirt road between Fredericksburg and Culpeper. It was run as a tent camp because the Madden's had far more overnighters than the tavern could hold—even sleeping three or four to a bed. Although blacks were not allowed to sell liquor, Mr. Maddens' family still has the bills for the great numbers of barrels of Rye whiskey consumed, by his family of course, at the same time receipts for overnight camping were high. The "new" tavern was built in 1840.[1]

This story illustrates the kind of personal view of history that I've gotten in many places on my trips. I mention it here as a major factor in developing my enthusiasm for traveling the country by motorcycle.

What follows is a summary of many memories and experiences. They are not in chronological order, but rather in the order in which they occurred to me, primarily stimulated by the locations I passed through during my current, (2003) trip. I recorded some notes about my memories as they occurred to me—on a small hand-held recorder. I've had so many interesting experiences over the years that now, as my friends will tell you, almost all my conversations bring to my mind some aspect or event from my motorcycle travels.

---

1.   Madden, T.O. *We Were Always Free*, Vintage Books, Random House, N.Y.

ORGANIZING MY MEMORIES

After each of my 43 annual trips I have written brief summaries of my "adventures" for my family and friends. These short stories have been primarily in the form of chronological sequences, "First I went to x, saw or did y and then went to z…" etc. much like the pattern of most travel stories. At age 80, remembering is a big thing and being able to enhance some fuzzy memories with these old records has revitalized my enjoyment of them.

So let's start with my last trip, July (2003), on the road north from my home in Lake of the Woods, Virginia—through Brandy Station, in a soft rain. I always claim that I enjoy the travel as much as being at the destination, but it wasn't so on the early part of this trip. The forecast predicted a week of severe thunderstorms throughout the east and I left in a drizzle. My wife, Marilyn had gone to visit with our daughter in Houston as she often does when I go on these trips. There she can worry about me with help from one of our daughters.

Trying to reset my somewhat dampened mood, I decided to use some memories to break through the gloom overhead—I was carrying my great little pocket sized "Sony Micro Dictator" to record some notes to help me to later write about the memories that I would have time to think about on the trip.

As usual, I had no tight schedule. And since my interpretation of the "Freedom" feeling includes being able to enjoy starting a trip without having a specific route or schedule in mind, I decided to wait until I could see if the various blue and gray profiles of the Blue Ridge Mountains got clearer before I decided on a route.

The morning's TV weather maps had shown vertical green blotches indicating thunderstorms separated by vertical yellow and orange (hot and sunny) blotches. I decided that as the days passed, I'd try to head generally north on, or toward, one of the sunny orange tiger stripes, fully aware that fast moving changes and irregularities in the weather pattern will probably arrange to soak me off any planned route choices almost every day.

And so they did. The light drizzle soon developed into a heavy rain.

On that hot rainy day I was wearing shorts with a tank top, and my old sneakers and no socks—always hoping the sun would eventually prevail.

It didn't. The rain got heavy, but it was too early to stop on my first day of the trip. It got so heavy that I couldn't see the road ahead, (no windshield wipers on motorcycles). I had to get off the road.

A PLACE TO START—AN UNLOCKED CAR

The visibility got to where I could barely see twenty feet ahead through my rain spattered windshield and rain-spotted glasses to find the edge of the road. I was down to about ten miles per hour and in fear of being hit from behind by some car or truck that had windshield wipers and might overtake me at 25-30 mph. I could have had better visibility if the whole world was under water.

I was reconsidering my descriptions of the pleasures of riding in the open air, when a big, green exit sign washed into my fuzzy view. With my left hand I took off my glasses, held them in my teeth and, with rain smacking my eyeballs, squinted to see enough of the white stripe on road's edge to help me creep off onto the "exit" road. I got off that road at the first opportunity. It turned out to be a Used Car lot.

The lot was closed, but I couldn't make myself go any further to find shelter. I sloshed up and down two rows of cars to find one unlocked. I found one, took off my muddy sneakers and crawled into the back seat. I pulled out my pocket recorder and started to dictate the outline of what is now Chapter Two, the story of my "Great Retirement Trip."

But it wasn't long before the release from the stress of riding blind, and the sound of rain on the car's roof got to me and I nodded off.

2

MY GREAT RETIREMENT TRIP

WILD ANTICIPATION

In the closing years of my working life,—the 1980s—I was making annual trips, but always fantasizing about riding on my motorcycle across the country with no constraints on my time and lots of opportunities to get acquainted with people who are different from our friends in the bureaucratic world of Washington.

Given the particular characteristics of motorcycle travel, I decided on three good ways to get acquainted.

One was to present myself as a man who worked with his hands rather than as a technical manager in a company funded by the government.

Another was to seek opportunities to work in a variety of jobs,—some for money and some that simply helped people with jobs they were doing themselves. I expected that my experience as an engineer and as a builder of my own home and having participated in building several Habitat houses should help me get work—especially since I had no concern about getting paid.

A third idea was to visit small town bars where, I had already learned, it's easy to get acquainted with local people if you arrive on a motorcycle.

We'll see how these three ideas worked out.

Marilyn, my wife, fretted about my day-dreaming during this "planning" period. She feels strongly that riding alone is unsafe, but getting involved with strangers is even more unsafe. (Funny thing though, she never seemed concerned about safety and always said she enjoyed riding with me during our courtship years. And, she gave up motorcycle riding the day we got married.)

As my retirement day came closer, I got noticeably more enthusiastic about the idea of tent camping across the country by motorcycle. Marilyn's anxiety grew at a similar pace. She wished that I would go fishing or hunting and playing golf in my free time "like all the other grown men." Finally, we agreed that I would sell the motorcycle in California and fly home and quit riding. But, as you will see, that agreement had to be renegotiated in Milwaukee, Wisconsin.

I finally left on the long planned trip in 1989, just after my 65th birthday and retirement party.

Overall, the weather was good and I tent-camped on most of the nights traveling through all the states between Virginia and North Dakota, through three Canadian Provinces and back through New England. I covered over 4000 miles and accumulated lots of bar and swimming-hole stories. And of course there had to be one colossal thunderstorm.

But first, let's talk a little about how I used employment as a way of making new friends.

WORKING MY WAY

One of the three ways mentioned above for getting acquainted with people was to find work along the way. I have always been fascinated by stories of men working their way across the country, mostly looking for work during the depression. Reading how they washed dishes in diners, chopped wood, did yard work or worked as farm hands, I decided to make seeking work a part of my trip plan. It turned out to be quite a challenge, but my three "strategies" worked well. I could not spend the time it takes to advertise in local papers or put up cards in stores, and then wait around for responses. But within the first week of my travel, I did succeed in getting an interesting mix of work-for-pay, I use the word "pay" rather loosely because the money never covered the bar bills associate with getting the jobs.

Two of the four jobs I got were negotiated in a Co-op store. Two others derived from bar conversations about what I was trying to do.

THE GRAIN ELEVATOR
(More new friends)

The first job I got was for a man I met in a Co-op Store in Farmington, Minnesota. I had set up my tent in a campground a little after noon and was at the counter of a nearby Co-op store asking if the store knew of anyone who had a job for an electrician. The conversation naturally led to me talking about my trip, and my need to take a break from daily riding. A couple of customers joined in with some questions and one of the men, who was the manager of a "granary" (a grain elevator) that buys, sells, and stores grain. He liked my offer to work for $20 for a day. He told me how to get to the granary from my campsite the next morning if I wanted to help unload some trucks bringing grain from farms to his granary.

I shoveled grain from farmer's trucks into a large tube that had a worm screw called a "spiral staircase" in it. The screw pushed the grain up about 30 feet to it spilled over into a silo-like storage tank. Between the arrivals of farmers with their grain, and

WORK IN A GRAIN ELEVATOR

when he wasn't drinking coffee with some who had finished unloading, the owner explained to me the use of a large chalk board that most farmers checked when they arrived with a load. It displayed current prices the government and some commercial outfits were offering for grain. I learned a bit about how the farmers decide whether to sell to the government, rent storage time or sell to the commercial operators who use the grain in a variety of products. Commodity prices change rapidly and some of the farmers don't decide on their options until they are actually at the granary.

It was obvious to me that the grain elevator operators are an intimate part of the local farm community. All conversations were on a first name basis and the granary manager spent much of the day drinking coffee with the guys who brought in the grain. After settling their paperwork, most would pour a cup and head for an old, partially disabled table where cream and sugar rituals got mixed with comments on "how's (name of wife) doin'?" In most cases the manager would then call me from my unloading operation to join them at the table to be introduced as a guy motorcycling his way to Saskatchewan. He'd follow that with his own ever increasingly embellished description of my traveling adventures. (At this point I had not worked for others on any of my trips, but I had ridden through much of Ontario, Quebec and Nova Scotia.)

THE TRACTOR REPAIRMAN
(A Farmer and a Coop Manager)

When I got back to the Co-op store to pick up my motorcycle after the days work in the granary, the counter man told me that he had mentioned to a local farmer that I was an available electrician. He put me in touch by phone with a farmer who needed someone to install an ignition harness on a tractor that wouldn't start. I took the job to make another twenty bucks.

The Co-op guy made the appointment for me and told me how to get to the farm the next morning.

It was hot. In the field the temperature was near a hundred degrees. I worked in shorts, which gave me sunburn problems for a day or two. The insulation on the tractor's old ignition harness was badly cracked and looked like it was 50 years old. It also looked like an animal had been chewing on the insulation! The farmer had already bought a new harness and plugs, mail ordered via the Co-op, but the harness didn't fit his old tractor. Nevertheless, I cut the lines to fit and reinstalled the cable terminal fittings using my knife and his plug wrench and pliers. And he had an old battery charger in his barn.

After installing the harness and plugs, charging up the battery and priming the carburetor with fresh gas, I drove the tractor in from the field to the happy owner who gave me a $5 tip on top of my pay of $20! Both of us felt real good about the transaction.

As you might have guessed his wife had made lemonade and invited me to supper. I was too smelly from the day in the field, but did sit with them an hour answering their questions about my travels.

With the $25 in my pocket and my sweat now dry, I felt like I now knew what 'Easy Livin' means. But I was anxious to get to the campground for a shower and to a bar near the Co-op for dinner.

THE ASSISTANT DELIVERY MAN
(Truck Driver)

It wasn't long before I was telling my Granary and Tractor stories at the bar and a man who said he heard about me at the Co-op offered me my third job. I was really on a roll! This time I accompanied a truck driver named Al Curry. My job was to load and unload goods from a big delivery truck which collected farm and small business products from rural locations and delivered them into Minneapolis.

I left my motorcycle in the Truck garage while we made his rounds. Most of his pickups were from small shed-like buildings or rebuilt barns. The drop-offs were mostly at warehouses and barns in and around Minneapolis which I took to be wholesalers who supported the city's retail businesses. Tomato paste was one product. Foldable bakery boxes were another. Specialized machine parts were a third. We also brought in a few crates of vegetables.

The route we traveled seemed to be a regular one for Al. He knew everyone at the pick up and delivery locations, not to mention all the people I had met on my two previous jobs. While I loaded or unloaded the cargo, he enjoyed drinking coffee with them and telling them all about me, while I unloaded stuff onto a hand truck and rolled it into the facilities. Once again I enjoyed the notoriety.

INVENTING A GARAGE DOOR OPENER
(A Pilot and Hanger Builder)

During the long trip to town in the truck and back, I exchanged a bit more personal information with Al, the driver, than I had time to do with the others I had met in the area. So during Al's coffee conversation at one of our drop off places, he mentioned that I was an engineer. As we finished unloading, the customer at one place who had become a friend of Al's told him that he had built his own airplane hanger and asked Al if we would come out to his home on the way back to Farmington to help him solve a problem with a big door he had built for it.

He had bought a garage door opener for a normal sized double door garage,—but it wasn't powerful enough to lift the very large hanger door that he had built. After much trading of ideas, we ran a cable from an eye-bolt at the bottom front of the door, up the outside of the door and over a 6-inch pulley mounted in a vertical slot we cut out in the wall above the door. We then ran the cable inside under the roof rafters to the center of the rear wall, over a second pulley and down to a swing-like board on which we could load cinder blocks. We put on just enough weight to assist the springs on the commercial door opener—so the door could be opened easily by the small half-horse motor.

I've made it sound simple, but try to imagine the wood work we had to do with two-by-fours to mount the two pulley axles. He had cable and clamps from the Co-op, but only small pulleys, too small to deal with the inflexible cable. Now comes the clever part. He had a child's small tricycle rusting in his house basement. We stripped the tires off of it and used two of its' wheels and their axle, cut in half to make the two "pulley" axles we needed. The first pulley had to be mounted in the slot we cut above the door so the cable remained outside and above the door and wouldn't interfere with the door as it curved into its open (horizontal) position. (The outside cable interfered with the top of the door opening when the door got wide open and started to pull the cable inside, but, fortunately, the door opened enough for the airplane to get in before the cable scraped the top door sill.)

The thing worked, but we needed some nuts and bolts in places we had used nails. We got back to my motorcycle very late. Al went back to work the next day, but I still had to go back with some needed hardware to finish the job and collect my "tip". By the time I got it done it was after lunch and too late to gather my tent and stuff and find another place. I decided to stay and camp here another night so I could get some addresses at the bar during supper. It turned out to be a good move.

A SPECIAL REWARD
(Three Country Families)

For me, these jobs had added an enjoyable chapter to my trip. The Tractor, Granary, and Airplane Hanger families I had "worked" for had become kind of personal friends. I returned to the campground to find a note from Al inviting me to a joint dinner with these three families at Al's house.

The three wives were well acquainted with most of the local people I had met. They knew all about the granary, tractor, and delivery truck and hanger door episodes. I was becoming a local gossip item, if not a celebrity. From their husbands they had heard about my travel stories, and when they heard I was headed for Saskatoon, they and their kids were crazy to see if I wore a coonskin hat and carried a long rifle. I had been eating bar food for days and the home cooked roast, corn, mashed potatoes and pie were a wonderful treat.

SOME ANXIETIES AT HOME

Now I had been about two weeks on the road enjoying these experiences, and reporting them (almost) daily in phone calls to my wife. As might be expected, she began to develop anxieties about what she considered my peculiar, if not abnormal, affection for my new lifestyle. Each evening's story about the series of four jobs made her a bit nervous—and the dinner party with the two families didn't help. Now remember—I was retired and she was still working full time. It wasn't hard to decode her feelings when she asked me if this was the way I planned to spend my time until she retired!

A ROMANTIC INTERLUDE

I decided it was time for us to talk things over, preferably in a nice country Inn for a few days. We arranged for her to fly to Milwaukee.

I left the motorcycle with a guy who had been on my ship in the war, one George Evans. He now lived in Madison, Wisconsin. I took a bus from his house to Milwaukee, and rented a car to meet Marilyn at the airport. I can still remember the mixture of excitement and anxiety and how my heart pounded when I met her at the plane. (It still happens.)

With the rented car we a spent a delightful four days together in and around a log cabin named the Everly House, built in 1844 on Hasmer Lake in Jackson, Wisconsin. We visited the "Historic Cedar Creek Settlement" just north of Milwaukee. We took pictures where the Barnum and Bailey wagons that are used in the annual Milwaukee Circus Parade (televised on NBC) are on display. And the timing was good for us to also attend the Wisconsin "Fish Day" celebration in Port Washington.

The result was a win-win renegotiation of my travel plans. You remember that our original agreement was that, on this great "retirement trip" I would cycle across the country from Virginia to California, sell the bike there, and fly home. Since she was giving me considerable pressure (and incentive) to come back home when I was only half way to California, we negotiated that I would go at least as far as Fargo, which is half way between Virginia and California—and then come back on a Canadian route across Ontario and Quebec into Maine and home to Virginia. And she agreed that since our first deal fell through, I would not be obliged to sell the motorcycle.

I was happy when I thought about how much more interesting my planned route was going to be than going on across Montana and down into southern California. The schematic map below shows the approximate distances between the main places that I visited after our "negotiation."

It should be obvious that her visit to Milwaukee had been good for both of us.

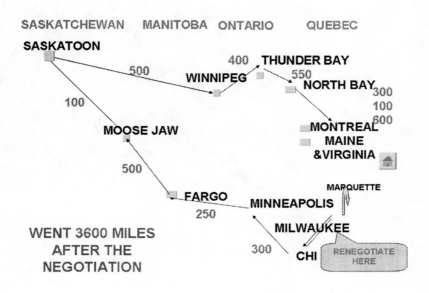

So we agreed that I would not tarry longer. I'd bus back to Madison to get my motorcycle, swing north for a swim in Lake Superior and then hurry on to

Ottawa, Illinois, to visit with her uncle. She felt that a visit with family would be a definite improvement in the nature of my travels.

It was only about 75 miles back to Madison where I left the bike with my old Navy buddy, George Evans. We hadn't seen each other since our part of the war ended in 1946, so we spent the evening talking about what's happened to us since then—our families, careers and my motorcycle travels.

George outlined a route for me to see Marquette and get a swim on the U.S. side of Lake Superior. He sent me on a NE diagonal course along Lake Winnebago and through Oshkosh to camp near Green Bay, Wisconsin. The next day it was a beautiful ride north along Lake Michigan, (route 35) before going on to Marquette.

It was early in the day when I got to Marquette. What I knew about it came from reading about Henry Ford's use of it as a gathering place for his famous friends. It was a major iron ore mining and shipping port then—and still ships iron ore, but now most visitors see it as a skiing center. Marquette Mountain is only an hour's flight from Chicago. Between the two times I visited there-20years apart, Sawyer AFB was closed and Sawyer International Airport replaced it.

In the bar I settled in, all the talk was about the period when Otto Preminger and a dozen very famous movie stars lived there while shooting a movie, *Anatomy of a Murder*, that won an Academy Award as Best Picture in the Oscar races. Seems much of the movie consisted of shots in local buildings. The bar tender insisted that it made the city famous.

Most of that night I was awake, re-living every minute of Marilyn's visit to see me in Milwaukee. So in the morning I took the swim to revive myself and switch my day dreams to the idea of going to Saskatoon instead of California. But part of our agreement was that I would first visit Marilyn's uncle in Ottawa, Illinois—and by now she would have advised him that I was on the way. Unfortunately, I had to go back south—the wrong way when you are trying to get to Fargo. (See my little map two pages back.) and little did I know that I would be causing a panic on the way. It turned out to be memorable for a lot of people.

CHAOS AT A GAS STATION
(No new friends at the truck stop.)

While I was traveling west from Chicago on route 80 toward Ottawa, Illinois, a horrendous thunderstorm came up. Along with several dozens of cars, I pulled into a Truck Stop to wait it out.

I was in the restaurant drinking coffee when a loudspeaker called for "someone who parked a motorcycle near the gas pumps." The manager was upset because my motorcycle, top heavy with luggage, had been blown over in the storm. He feared that gas might be leaking from the motorcycle tank and that someone in one of the many parked cars with idling motors and cigarette smokers in them might toss out a cigarette and ignite the gas and blow up the whole complex!

I ran out to my sad bike, which was lying helpless in the pouring rain. Fortunately the gas tank wasn't leaking and no gas was spilled. But I couldn't lift the motorcycle up. I had to unload the camping equipment that had to be untied first. I got it half done before a young man in a kitchen chef-type outfit came out and helped me lift it up. After I moved the cycle around back away from the pumps and went back in the restaurant to try and dry out, I found myself facing a hostile crowd. They were frightened by the manager's announcement about a dangerous explosion and had watched the whole affair.

The crowd decided that the young chef was a hero, risking his life like that, and that I was a typical no-brains, motorcycle rider who needlessly risked the lives of hundreds of people. Nevertheless, the manager gave the young chef and me a much appreciated cup of coffee.

Having so much camping stuff on the bike had once before caused me embarrassment. On bad days in recent years, I sometimes had trouble climbing into the small sitting space between the luggage on the back and a small leather bag strapped on top of the gas tank. (More about this in Chapter Eight) Years ago I could do the Roy Rogers "leap-frog" thing the way he mounted Trigger. But I quit it when one day I forgot there was a camera in the tank bag. A sensitive part of me I landed on it.

Well, on to Ottawa and a pleasant evening telling my wife's uncle about my adventures since leaving home. I used his garage to change the oil in the motorcycle and check valve settings. Then we went to "Zellers" bar for Manhattans. Zellers bar has a brass foot-rail mounted on the floor between the bar and the bar stools. Under the foot rail there is a channel of flowing water that patrons used to spit their chewing tobacco into. Today it's a popular attraction.

From Ottawa I headed north to find a campsite in the Wisconsin Dells, a beautiful and popular vacation area. I came upon a sort of ranch where people stayed in cabins, ate in a "mess hall", tended their own horses in the proprietor's stables, and rode horses in groups all day long. The nature of the facility made me curious, and the food smelled inviting, so I got a room for the night in the main lodge and spent the evening getting acquainted with some of the "horse people" who happened to be almost as interested in motorcycles as they were in horses. It seems they never leave their horses home alone. They chose places like this to spend their vacations, places with stables, riding trails, feed and horse-washing facilities and places to park their horse trailers. They were all up and starting out on the trails when I got to breakfast the next day.

MY TEEPEE NEAR FARGO, NORTH DAKOTA
A policeman and some Indians

I now headed for North Dakota, the "Sioux State."

Fargo was a big disappointment. It's the largest city in the state, and Sturbridge nothing like what we saw in the old Western movies. (Most of the roads are paved now.) It's a legendary place named after a famous stagecoach line, but I couldn't find a bar with swinging doors where cowboys would be playing poker with bare shouldered bar girls looking on,—or for that matter, any signs of the towns' history.

I told a friendly policeman about my disappointment and asked him what happened to the Sioux Indians who originally owned the territory. He referred me to the Pioneer Village & Museum in Bonanzaville, West Fargo, where for a couple of bucks I took "a stroll back in time." But the stroll wasn't long enough. The Village consisted of several blocks of colonial buildings, including a church, a schoolhouse, a blacksmith, etc. much like many "authentic living museums" I have seen in other states. Ford's Greenfield Village in Dearborn, Michigan, Williamsburg in Virginia and Sturbridge, Village in Massachusetts, and a dozen less sensational places, come immediately to mind.

The policeman picked up on my interest in Indians and suggested that if I wanted to meet some Indians, I should try a certain bar outside of town where some of them hung out.

The bartender there pointed me to a guy they called the "Chief," sitting with a couple of his brothers, at one of the tables. A big guy in dungarees and a dirty T-shirt, he was big enough that if he said he was the Chief, nobody was going to question it. They were not aware that I had arrived on a motorcycle with Virginia plates on it, so I needed method number two to open a conversation. Being something of a primitive myself, I approached the small tribes' table and stood with a beer in my hand hoping to be invited to join them, and asked if they knew where I could get some electrical work. One of them suggested that I ask the workers at a nearby construction site where a row of houses was being built.

Naturally one of them went on to ask me where I was from. So I gave the group some version of my trip from Virginia. After a couple of them told their own Harley Davidson stories, the guy called Chief explained that the group was the remnants of a small Sioux tribe who shared a modest income from an oil company that had a lease on some "tribal" lands. Oil was discovered in North Dakota in 1951. Since the Indians still held some land and they didn't like farming, they turned to full time oil check-cashing and casino-planning.

After we shared a couple of beers, and were kind of groping for more to talk about, one of the "tribe" at the table said that the Chief had a son who once had a brief "affair" with a young Moose. (Use your imagination). The son is now a big guy and his Indian name is "Big Moose."

Now here comes the hard part; Big Moose has maintained a close relationship with the Moose he had "befriended" when he was young, and this moose "friend" is now a kind of ring leader of the local moose who hang out around Fargo. In fact, they said, Big Moose has a job working for the Fargo Chamber of Commerce. He works from 8 a.m. to 10 pm, down on Queen's Highway 417 directing a small group of moose friends, led by his special moose friend, to walk along the Highway to frighten, and generate memories, for tourists.

The more interest I showed in the crazy story, the more they embellished it—as if they had told it so many times that they each had a segment to offer. It was getting dark outside, and in the spirit of bar conversation, I thought I was being humorous when I asked if any of them had any Teepees to rent for the night. Surprise! One of them said yes, he had one teepee open—"sleep in your own bedroll." In keeping with the rest of the baloney that had been going down, one of the "tribe" now offered that the last teepee he rented had turned into a disaster. "While a renter was sleeping in it, a Moose started eating it, and it was the only teepee I had for tourists!" Another guy added that the renter had departed swiftly while the Moose was eating the tent and never did pay for the part of the night he slept before the Moose arrived for a snack.

With my sleeping arrangements now established, I sat around waiting for Big Moose to get "home from work." I heard a little about their involvement in the dancing ceremonies these guys do at several tourist traps around Fargo, but the beer was making me sleepy. The teepee I slept in turned out to be a sort of commercial "sign" used to attract people to some sort of commercial operation. After I accepted his offer, the Chief went on to tell me about the troubles he was having with the city fathers in Fargo concerning how the sewer codes and regulations should be interpreted, He said that the tent-eating incident was the last straw, the one that made him decide to get out of the teepee renting business. Besides, he said, "teepee renters are a strange breed."

RENTED TEE PEE

They all enjoyed this pulling of my leg, (and each others), and I assume they are still talking about the Virginia guy on the motorcycle who actually believed their stories. Two good things came out of it. One, I wound up in my bedroll in a teepee, a situation not very different from what I was used to in my own tent. And two, Fargo turned out to be one of the most fun evenings on my trip.

About seven the next morning the road traffic about thirty feet from the teepee woke me up. I rode back to the bar for some coffee and to pay for my lodging. The bartender was cleaning up. He said, "No charge. The Chief paid your tab." I interpreted this as quiet appreciation for the fun evening we enjoyed together—and pretty good evidence that none of them actually owned the tent. I asked if Big Moose or the Chief were around so I could say good bye. He said with smile that I might see them on "tourist-scaring duty" down the road.

INTO CANADA

I headed northwest through Minot and across the Canadian border toward Moose Jaw, watching cautiously for 'Meese'. I couldn't help but wonder if I might have passed where Big Moose and his moose friends were working for the Chamber of Commerce, but I scolded myself for even thinking that any part of what the Indians had told me could actually be true. Anyway, as I mulled over all they told me the fun of last night and enjoyed the feel and hum of my engine, I unconsciously picked up speed on the lonesome road. I had to be doing around 70 mph when I saw the flashing red light in my rear view mirrors.

By the time the trooper caught me I had my speed down to around 55, but the Trooper didn't take out his ticket pad! He couldn't tell that I'm a pitiable old man because I was wearing my helmet and sun glasses. He simply said, "Son, you've got to slow down. The Moose here are so used to tourists that it's not unusual for them to step out of the woods in front of a speeder just for the fun of it. If one steps out in front of that motorcycle, you're dead. Now go ahead, but keep your speed down." Then he made a U-turn and headed back to one of the secret places that all troopers emerge from, to do whatever troopers do behind the road signs and in other hiding places.

The courtesy of the Trooper made me wonder. Was Big Moose for real or had the Chief sent the Trooper out so I would believe his "dangerous moose" story.

SASKATOON AND THE MÉTIS

The trooper's friendliness and the cooler air slowly cleared my head. I stopped only once on the hour trip to camp near Minot. Next morning I used my Virginia's driving license for I.D. as I crossed the border into Saskatchewan, one of the "Prairie Provinces" of Canada.

After catching up on the breakfast I had missed, I passed through Moose Jaw, once a major Indian Trading Post, later a rustic small town rail hub—and now a modern city. I didn't stop. I wanted to make it to Saskatoon by the next day.

I got to Saskatoon in the afternoon of the next day. It turned out to be no more of a remote outpost than Fargo was. What was once a trapping, farming, lumbering and fishing center is now a distribution center for produce and livestock for the whole province. Its railroads, grain elevators, oil refineries, meatpacking plants, stockyards, manufacturing plants and all kinds of businesses, are all interwoven with new construction. The city now boasts hotels, museums, a Zoo, a Symphony Orchestra, river cruises on the Saskatchewan River, Police and Fire Departments, tour buses and tour boats are all over the place. It's just another city; the kind I usually like to bypass! But ever since my daughter, Rhonda, worked for Frontier Airlines, and couldn't get me a free ticket to Saskatoon, I had wanted to go there. I liked the name of the place and had read a bit about its history.

To find someone to talk to—and at the same time learn a little more about local history, I checked in at the Chamber of Commerce Tourist Office. Everyone there knew all about the commercial activities of the city, nightlife, restaurants, etc.—but they had some trouble finding someone who could talk about some of the history of the region. The man they found assumed I wanted to hear about current events and immediately got into local politics. But with a little coaxing he transitioned into the current issues relating to policies concerning the hundreds of what the Canadians consider their minorities. They are descendants of Aboriginal tribes who intermarried with Canadian fur trappers called "Voyageurs." They were later granted "First Nations" status. They are commonly called "Half Breeds."[1]

Now if you couldn't care less about Canadian history, skip ahead to page 27 where I leave Saskatoon, where is says AFFAIR WITH A MAN WITH A CROSS. But remember that I told you in the Introduction that getting to know people involves talking about what interests them.

The First Nations have lots of committees, like our own Bureau of Indian Affairs. While their politicians seem to focus on their social status, my impression was that their real focus is on negotiating their claims for compensation for what lands their forefathers lost, the territories called "Crown Lands". Although their claims are based in a substantial body of fuzzy paperwork, their loss struck me as a lot like that of the American Indians when Americans found out there was gold or oil or even good farming on their Reservations.

Saskatoon is a sort of crossroads of a half dozen histories. It was the eastern edge of the territory where the early French trappers and Voyageurs married Indians and established a unique culture of "Half Breeds," called "Métis." (Pronounced "May-teece") Before roads and train tracks came in, the Métis provided canoe and back-pack transport of furs and related supplies between Montreal and western Canada, focusing in an area called the Red River area, now Manitoba.

After the British took Quebec and Ontario from the French (they already had taken the Maritime Provinces) they, the British, decided to buy the lands belonging to their own British Hudsons Bay Company—the lands where the Métis had set up homesteads and communities. The Métis, seeing their homes being taken, tried to block the British importation of Scots and Irish that were brought in to convert the Buffalo-rich Métis lands into farms. History now calls the Métis resistance an Insurrection. (Today's Métis include many Scottish and Irish families descendant from the intermarriage of Indians with the first groups the British brought in to establish farms and communities the British could control.)

Here near Saskatoon, the Métis also fought the penetration of the French Northwest Company penetrating from the east. Next the Hudson Bay Company (British) fought the French Northwest Company—until they merged! Then the Canadian Pacific Railroad sent an army in. You want to talk about an exciting location?

Through all these battles the Métis lost their homesteads and lands. Their "insurrection" leader, Louis Riel, was executed. But today they still exist as a semi-organized minority voice in Canada, with representation in the Canadian Parliament.

---

1.   Scofield, Gregory. *Thunder Through My Veins*. HarperCollins Publishers Ltd.

After my chat with the Chamber of Commerce guy I got a room in a Holiday Inn with the kind of businessman's bar you find in all Holiday Inns. Sure enough, the only guys I got to talk to were the bar tender who knew no history and the guys in business suits on the bar stools next mine. Although my Virginia license plates attracted enough attention to generate conversations into the late evening, I couldn't find anyone interested in the Métis history.

The next day I got up itchy with indecision about which way to go. I decided on the Queen's Highway 16 east, and a long ride to the huge city of Winnipeg, Capital of Manitoba. I got a motel before reaching the city, swam some laps in the indoor pool and watched a Chamber of Commerce TV channel program about the city. They have traffic problems.

In the morning I spent my usual half hour cleaning and worshiping my motorcycle for its faithful and magnificent performance over the past few weeks before I headed east for Thunder Bay, Ontario, with no idea that it would lead me to one of the most interesting meetings I have ever experienced.

AN AFFAIR WITH A MAN AND A CROSS
An evangelist

I left Thunder Bay heading east along the north side of Lake Superior, blissfully unaware that anything interesting lay ahead. Somewhere around a place called Marathon, I was cruising along while daydreaming and feeling a bit lonesome, when I saw, up ahead of me a cross. It was on a man's back! And he was peddling a bicycle!

I coasted to a stop a little way ahead of him so he could adjust to the shock of seeing another live human being. He coasted up next to me.

He was dressed in a loose and dirty white robe, something like an old night-shirt, and he had a large wooden cross tied to his back! A small bundle of possessions was rolled up in what looked like a very small bedroll and was strapped behind the saddle of the bicycle. He was thin and bony and looked like he wouldn't get much further without a meal. His hair was long and his hollow eye sockets were partially hidden behind unruly face hair and the scrubby beard that spread over most of his face.

The cross looked heavy. It seemed to be made of two pieces from about a four inch tree trunk. A (roughly) three foot vertical member was tied to a two foot cross piece. Neither piece had been sawed lengthwise, so it looked like he had made it while on the road, i.e. crummy.

It occurred to me that he might be Arthur Blessitt; the guy shown in this picture. Some magazine told me has been carrying a 12 foot cross around the globe for over 20 years. He's the guy who in the mid 1980's according to some reports,[2] led George W. Bush to accept Christ.

But I've since looked up Blessitt (shown in this picture). He dragged that big cross with a small wheel on the bottom. The guy I met wasn't Blessitt.

The first thing he said was that he was very pleased that I stopped. He said he had been wondering what purpose the Lord had for this day—and that our meeting was the Lord's his answer. The Lord arranged for us to meet. I supported his thesis, saying—quite truthfully—that I too had been wondering what the hell I was doing so far from the real world for the past couple of days.

Without me having to ask, he explained that *he was following the trail that Jesus trod after He (Jesus) came to America following His resurrection!* He said Jesus came up into Canada after planting the gospel in the Indian Tribes of America. (Some of you, like me, may not have known about this.) In Canada Jesus supposedly selected some disciples, one of whom was this man himself. He said that Jesus "called" him and explained that he, like Saint Paul, was "called by the Spirit," while on the road, and that he was charged to preach the gospel to Canada. I thought to myself that it wasn't much different than the revelations the Mormons claim started their church[3].

As he talked, some Old Testament verses I knew from Handel's Messiah came to my mind, "...get thee up into the high mountain! Lift up thy voice! Lift it up, be not afraid!"

2.   Dickinson, Tim. *Prayer for W.* Mother Jones Magazine dated December-January, 2006 article *April 1984*

3.   Smith, Joseph. *The Book of Mormon.* The Church of Jesus Christ of Latter Day Saints, Salt Lake City, Utah, USA

His recommended road to salvation was of course New Testament oriented (John 3:16 etc.) I can't remember how he put it, but it was not unlike another verse Handle had used in the Messiah:

Him to me: "Lift up your head(s), be ye lifted up, ye everlasting doors, and the King of Glory shall come in!"

Me to him: "Who is the King of Glory?"

Him: "The Lord of Hosts, He is the King of Glory!"

Me to him: "I'm a Baptist myself, and it isn't for one second just because I happened to be born one" (I remembered this explanation from Sinclair Lewis' The Man Who Knew Coolidge[4])

Of course he wouldn't settle for this. While he remained standing holding his bicycle up, his well intentioned spiel went on with no acknowledgement that I had responded. It was so continuous and predictable that it made me impatient. I was dying to ask him about where he would shelter that night, or how he got food, bed or sex, but I couldn't make myself interrupt him. But after maybe ten minutes of listening, I mounted my motorcycle and started the motor to signal that I wanted to end his pitch before he transitioned into the "won't you accept" phase or the inevitable "let us pray together" phase. He started forward as if to accompany me—and continued his sermon.[5]

He had no tent, and we seemed to be a long way from any kind of lodging on bleak Queen's Highway 17. His bike had no light and the highway had none either! I had to interrupt him with some dumb statement like "Thank you for the fellowship, but I've got to leave now" and eased away as he said something about having planted a seed, and that "God will be continuing to contact me." He was right. God did.

It was only after I left him that the heavy emotional impact of the meeting began to invade me. No doubt he's still "up there" somewhere. As he faded in my rear view mirrors, I imagined his theme was "I will cling to the old rugged cross, and exchange it someday for a crown..." I thought to myself "there goes another true zealot, a man fully defined by a single purpose,—to get another jewel in his crown, a man exempt from reason or rationality, or even common sense." But I will be coming back to talk about him again later.

---

4.   Lewis, Sinclair. *The Man Who Knew Coolidge*, Books for Libraries, 1971
5.   In trying to identify this man by using the web, I found dozens of similar experiences listed under "Man carrying a Cross" Two men were arrested in Dayton Tenn. for "disturbing the piece" by dragging crosses. An "Irish Evangelist" is carrying one on a bicycle from Cal. to N.Y. Dozens of others are listed. It looks like Blissett inspired a great following.

About an hour further down the road I came to the small town of Marathon, Ontario. It had a restaurant and a couple of motels to house the hunters, fishermen and snowmobilers who like remote areas. But after filling my stomach, I got some guidance from my waitress, and rode a couple of miles further east to pay $4.00 and set up my tent in Pukaskwa National Park, right on the shores of Lake Superior—almost half way between Thunder Bay and Sault Ste Marie.

After a cool swim I sat by a picnic table with a warm Irish whiskey and thought about walking back on route 17 to see if a bicycle might be in sight. But I didn't want to be seen walking around with a whiskey bottle and I didn't want to set it down. I sat and watched the road. He didn't show up.

About five hours or riding the next day got me to North Bay, Ontario.

LONESOME IN NORTH BAY

Having just had a thousand mile ride from Saskatoon, and a kind of sobering conversation with the guy with the cross on his back, I was feeling tired and lonesome. The gloom was severe enough that I checked the North Bay Railroad Station to see if I could get passage to anywhere in the U.S. They said I'd have to drain my motorcycle's gas and oil and have the bike crated, before they could ship it. Of course there was no place in North Bay that would crate it. I thought of the embarrassment, along with a touch of shame that would come from interrupting my great motorcycle adventure with the bike and me crated on a train. I decided to get a room in one of the old motels that once housed crowds of visitors who came to see the Dionne Quintuplets.

So I spent the evening reading a book about Yvonne, Cecile, Annette, Emilie and Marie—and the next morning hearing the same stories from the motel manager in exchange for some of my motorcycle stories.

THE QUINTUPLETS

The famous Dionne Quintuplets were born here in 1934, when North Bay was still a tiny settlement. The controversial Doctor Allan Dafoe, who delivered them, removed them from their family and arranged that they be made wards of the Ontario government under his supervision. He then exploited their notoriety in a virtual theme park called "Quintland." The local tourist information says that "as many as 6,000 visitors a day came to watch the girls at play! They became a huge commercial enterprise, selling endorsements for hundreds of products..."

In the motel I got a book about the Quintuplet story from the motel desk, a book called "Family Secret"[6]. I read about the girls sexual abuse by their father, that the girls eventually sued the government for a share of the money that North Bay and Dr. Dafoe made from tourists and that the first three girls survived to enjoy a $4 million compensation award from the Ontario government in 1988. Even as I read the Soucy book in bed, I felt distracted by the "lonesome feeling" that had been with me since soon after I left Saskatoon. After my warm conversation in the library with the Métis gentleman, I had no real contact with people other than those at motel sign-in desks like the one here in North Bay. As I mentioned to the man with the cross, there have been times since I entered Canada that I have felt the "What am I doing here!" feeling. It was probably the several days of hard riding from Saskatoon to North Bay without friendly human contact that had brought me to this state of mind. I don't recall that it ever happened to me in the U,S. I started looking forward to crossing the border into Maine.

The night's rest brought me back to my sense of happiness that comes from looking forward to seeing what a new day will have to offer.

NO LUCK WITH MY FRENCH
Some French people.

Since I had toured Ontario several times over the years (see Chapter Ten), I continued another hundred miles on the fast Highway (17) east from North Bay through Ottawa and just beyond Montreal to a campground in a place called Cookshire, near the small town of Sherbrooke, Quebec. It was about 40 miles from the Maine border on "Birchton-Route" 108.

According to the map, the campground had a lake, and, after another four hundred mile high speed day from North Bay, I was looking forward to a relax-

---

6.   Soucy, Jean-Yves, *Family Secrets.* March 30,1997 G.T.Putman's Sons

ing swim in it. But I ran into what in my weary state felt like a brick wall at the camp's entrance. I paused a minute to practice saying, "Bonjour. Je suis désolé, mais je ne parle pas français." ("Hello. I'm sorry, but I do not speak French.") It looked proper in the book, but came out sounding like "Jesus is alone in the parlor pissing on France."

No one at the gate spoke English and after hearing my French the desk man got nervous, couldn't figure where I was from and wouldn't let me register. I tried to waving my credit card in one hand while pointing the other to outside the door and down to my Virginia license plate and then up to my camping luggage, but he watched me waving my arms and just shook his head nervously. I thought he might be reaching for a weapon, so I backed out the door, left my motorcycle and walked into the campground. I still couldn't find anyone who would talk to me. If they understood me, they would not acknowledge it.

It was too remote a location and too late in the day for me to consider looking for another place. I stood by my bike, shunned by all, snubbed by a few, feeling like some kind of untouchable,—tempted to just ride in and set up my tent. But some God sent help. It must have had something to do with the man with the cross. One of the campers came up to the gate from the outside. He looked at my loaded motorcycle, noticed my Virginia license plates and my forlorn look, smiled through his half open car window and asked me *in English* "Do you need some help?" I didn't drop to my knees in gratitude because I was afraid it might scare him off.

He got me registered and explained that the campground owner just wouldn't deal with Americans or other crazy people unless they spoke French—or just laid some Canadian money on the counter. He wouldn't accept charge cards or American money, but fortunately, I had enough Canadian money.

After I separated from the Good Samaritan, I set up my tent, but then found that there was no toilet paper in the bathrooms and no one would give or sell me any. One couple I asked just stood with a roll of it in their hand and pointed to the main gate. I didn't know if this meant "go back to America with the rest of the crazies" or "maybe they have some up front." Exhausted from the long ride, the trouble at the gate, no supper, setting up the tent and a growing need for a bathroom, I flopped on my bedroll to think things over.

Kidding aside, the attitude of these campers troubled me a lot. I enjoy making friends with people and just couldn't break the ice here. I knew the tensions between the English and French were strong in Montreal where the English speaking people tend to dominate the economic life of the city and the French don't like it. Lying in the tent, I got to thinking about it in engineering terms.

1. We've all heard that the French (Cartier) claimed "Canada" as a colony of France in the 1500s. (Canada means "a group of huts" in the Indian language.) They called it "New France."

2. A hundred years later, France got nervous that its Colony might intermix with the crazy British, Italian, Spanish and maybe even some Protestants in the British colonies a few miles south, so they shipped a big load of Frenchmen into New France, and made it a "Province" called Quebec. OK so far?

FRENCH CAMPGOUND

3. Then, as I learned in Saskatoon, the British took note of the prosperous fur trade the French voyageurs had started in the west, and their British Hudson Bay Company muscled in. The British King (George III) also smelled more money in the natural resources of Canada. He also heard rumors that the rebels in Boston were coaxing Quebec to help them kick the British out of America. So to get control of the situation, George decided to help the western (Canadian) Indians take Quebec (the French and Indian War)

4. The British took Quebec just a dozen years before the U.S. declared our Independence.

5. Now here's the dumb part. The Protestant English King refused to give the conquered French of Quebec a say in governance because they were Roman Catholics! Ha! No wonder they wouldn't share their toilet paper with me. No wonder they dislike anyone who isn't French!

Before this trip I thought that the familiar touch of haughtiness or lofty detachment that is found in many of the French of Europe came from their nation's history as conquerors and "rulers" of Europe in the Napoleonic era, when military achievements brought glory and "honor" to conquerors—things that the non-French are supposed to learn to respect (forever).

It was now dark outside. My big analysis had made me forget that I had to pee. In my under shorts I sneaked through the dark to the campground toilet.

Don't ask for details. I then took a swim in my shorts and stumbled in the half light of campground fires and Colman Lanterns, back to my tent. No supper.

ROADSIDE CAMP IN ONTARIO

In the morning I noted that the campground was really quite attractive. The camp sites were small, but very neat and tidy. There was a sense of permanency about it. Many campsites had a bench at the front and flower beds around the property lines. Some sites had trellis arches laced with flowers over their lot entrances. It was obviously a more or less closed community of families that stayed there for the summer. Mostly women and children. The husbands commuted on week ends from jobs in Montreal. No one was interested in trying to converse with a guy on a motorcycle, a guy who can tell wonderful stories, but a guy who is partially crazy, doesn't wear a beret and doesn't speak French.

I left early—with my wet shorts wrapped in a towel on top of a wet tent. No, I didn't pee on the tent. It was dew. I passed through La Patrie and about 20 miles later on a completely uninhabited back road, went on east to cross an isolated border into Maine. It was unmanned and labeled the "Coburn Gate," one of only two connections on the couple of hundred mile border between Quebec and Maine. (Shows how friendly we are with that part of Canada.)

Having missed dinner and breakfast at the French camp, I now had to travel another hour through dense Maine woods, on a road of course—on route 27 if you must know, before I finally reached a gas station and a good and homey breakfast place in Stratton, Maine.

While eating breakfast, I checked my maps and thought about what things I should see in Maine. Two things came to mind: the L.L. Bean store and Old Town, where their famous canoes are made.

OLD TOWN CANOES
Two old canoe makers.

This place took me half way back to the good old days when I made a try at canoeing every river in New York State. I lived on Lake Delta in Rome, N.Y., near the southern end of the Adirondacks' Fulton Chain of (mostly) connected lakes. The chain is named after Robert Fulton who tried to locate a canal route from the Great Lakes to the Hudson River. After canoeing through the 130 mile chain from Old Forge to Plattsburg, I bought a 1956 book called Canoeable Waterways of New York State by Lawrence I. Grinnell[7]—and began a long series of canoe trips with a friend to update Grinnell's descriptions of New York's rivers. The longest trip was a couple of hundred miles down the Susquehanna from above Cooperstown, N.Y. to Havre de Grace, Maryland. I carried the paddle with me on my overnight stops. Like the motorcycle, it was helpful in making conversation with new acquaintances.

In this age of plastic Kayaks and paddle boats, I still love canoes. In Old Town the wood smell in the old buildings adds to the pleasure of seeing the canoes constructed. They showed me some production data that goes back to 1903. They were producing between 200 and 400 canoes a month a hundred years ago! In 1910, they built 3500 and most people who have one consider it a treasure. Having its canoes viewed as treasures is good for Old Town, because plastic and aluminum canoes are a lot cheaper.

Generally speaking, I've found that Maine people are not much for small talk, but they do ask questions. Once again my motorcycle and its Virginia license plates got me a chat with a couple of old timers sitting on a bench and smoking their pipes near the canoe factory where my bike was parked. They worked for the canoe factory all their lives and neither one had made a long trip by canoe. "Don't have the time" they said. They also commented that they found it hard to imagine a person who loved canoeing being interested in motorcycles. Hmmm. They each had a canoe, (probably from a big employee discount deal) but only for family use on the quiet river that runs through town.

I hadn't slept well in the French Camp, so I called my wife for help. She checked the web and booked me into a motel in Bangor, where I enjoyed a good lobster dinner.

---

7.   Grinnell, Lawrence, *Canoeable Waterways of NY State, 1956* Pageant Press NYC

THE L.L.BEAN STORE

The next day I got down to Freeport where what's called "the Flagship LL Bean store" attracts hundreds of tourists and shoppers, mostly outdoorsmen and your standard female shoppers, from all over the world. I especially like their camping section, but always look at the prices of their "Bean Boots"—the combination rubber shoe stitched to a leather top—looking kind of like the "spats" we wore in the Navy. In 1911 this single handmade product got started in Mr. Bean's basement as a mail order business, and is now an international phenomenon. I'm sure that every camper, fisherman and hunter in the world knows of the Bean catalog and its rugged products, including Old Town Canoes.

I had to observe as I climbed back on my motorcycle, how much I'm attracted to the people who shop in Beans—and how "junky" my stuff looks compared with what I saw in the store. Just looking at the Bean product line gives me the impression that it appeals to the kind of people who, to a large extent, favor what is natural, practical, functional and made to last, rather than what is strictly stylish or fashionable. It's the outdoor people as distinct from those who have to dress and act in accordance with what has been defined as "proper" for a "cultural" environment, i.e. one without any motorcycles other than those belonging to Malcolm Forbes or Jay Leno.

It was now afternoon and hot. I was again running out of steam. Those long runs all across Canada must have sapped my energy. It had been a really nice ride from the French Campground to breakfast in Maine, and I had spent a pleasant hour at the Old Town Canoe place, but the fast and hot run down 95 to Freeport seemed to do me in. And although I had a midnight swim in the French Campground lake last night, I needed a bath. I found in my camping book a place called the Red Apple Campground just outside of Kennebunkport—and only about 40 miles south of Bean's—but on 95 again. At the Red Apple I got a shower and washed my clothes in their laundry room, and a good night's rest in their tenting section—without even trying to make new acquaintances...other than telling a few French Campground stories in the men's shower and ladies washer dryer room.

KENNEBUNKPORT AND HUMMING WHALES

I woke to a beautiful sunny morning and after my "free" continental breakfast, I washed my mud covered motorcycle with a towel—after all, Mr. Busch might see it and want a ride! I got instructions on how to get a drive-by look at President

Busch's nearby Kennebunkport compound. It was worth seeing through the hedges, but no tours were offered. So I parked the bike on a side street and shopped around the town's tourist traps awhile, took a few photos of the boats and yachts in the harbor before heading west through Hopkinton to Sunapee, New Hampshire.

Some whale voice interpreters

I stopped for a swim in Lake Sunapee and a visit with friends from Boston who had a summer place on lake. They had three of their friends there and after we all had a swim, we ate cheese sandwiches in their country kitchen and retired to the living room for an hour of my travel tales. The weary group then got to listening to recordings of whales making noises that my friends said were whale conversations. When this went on for several minutes, it dawned on me that they had been passing a cigarette around, not talking much—just listening to the whales and sort of daydreaming—with an occasional self-oriented smile as they seemed to latch on to something profound in the Whale conversations.

I felt a bit restless and tried to think of a graceful way to depart. Early on when I called them from Freeport, my friends had invited me to stay the night. And now it occurred to me that all afternoon the whales had been considering this. I began to forget that these were only recordings and to wonder if I was intruding in some kind of communications ritual. But the whales certainly weren't making any special effort to get their views on the matter through to me.

I took the bull by the horns, stood up and said that I felt the urge to take a moonlight ride on this beautiful and clear summer night. Nobody moved. They all kind of smiled and said different versions of "Right On!" and "Way Out!" I picked up my stuff that I had brought in—thinking I was staying for the night—but Before I got them tied back on the bike, one guy, Ken, came out and said he thought my idea was "great!" He said he had a motorcycle and a friend with a place in Cambridge, Mass. who he could call, so we could take the moonlight ride (around a hundred miles) and sleep when we got to Cambridge. He rolled out a motorcycle from somewhere and off we went.

A MOONLIGHT RIDE

The skies were crowded with the a million stars and a bright moon—the kind of night one only seems to find only in the mountains. Side by side on the vacant road, we had a fantasy four hour ride down from the mountains to Cambridge, Mass, No conversation. No traffic. No lights but those on our bikes, and the bright moon. We met a little traffic in Concord and on the Manchester bypass, but overall it was a magical, ride.

After a couple of shots of scotch and a couple of hours of sleep at Ken's friend's house in Cambridge we took a walk around the Harvard Yard and enjoyed breakfast in a place near the Yard that was crowded with students—one where they assume you are "faculty" if you have a touch of grey hair and don't order "the breakfast special."

After breakfast Ken and I split and I went a couple of miles toward downtown Boston, to stop at MIT. It's tough to find a parking place around where thousands of students have cars, but it's easy to squeeze in a motorcycle almost anywhere.

I like to read the bulletin boards and posters that the students put on the walls of all the halls between the classroom doors. Party schedules, text books for sale, openings for another renter at a community-type arrangement, opportunities to share a ride to N.Y., etc. are posted on papers that have tabs cut into their edges so those interested can simply tear off a tab with the appropriate phone number rather than have to write it down.

A college Professor

I knew the office location of a Professor who I had worked with for about a year on a Department of Transportation project in Washington, so I checked it out. By luck he was there and very curious about my life after retirement. To me he seemed retired-in-place. We spent an hour trading information about how our project spawned world peace, how hard it was to get government money these days and what his prospects were for leaving MIT and going to work for a living. (I think he subsequently took a job at the Department of Transportation in Washington.)

After too much coffee with him in the campus cafeteria—on top of the coffee I had earlier in Cambridge, I spent a little time in the Campus Student Union looking for good book prices and trying to decide where to head for. Home seemed to dominate my thinking.

I made the 500 mile ride to Virginia, mostly with knees squeezed together around the gas tank to minimize the number of multiple pee stops that the coffee stimulated. From Cambridge south I enjoyed such "fun" landmarks as pieces of the Massachusetts Turnpike, the Taconic Parkway, the Tappan Zee bridge, the Interstate and Garden State Parkways, the New Jersey Turnpike, the Delaware Memorial bridge, the Baltimore Harbor Tunnel and Washington's Beltway.

I had ridden over 4400 miles. Clearly, I was ready to bring to a close my "Great Retirement Trip."

3

LIFE IN THE COUNTRY

That "Great Retirement Trip" was thirteen years ago. Some of you will remember from Chapter I that a good part of this book was started in 2003 when I dictated an outline of that spectacular trip while sitting in an empty car on a used car lot waiting for the rain to stop. That long outline was followed by a good snooze.[1]

When I woke up, the rain was down to a drizzle. Since the rain had lightened up, I fish-tailed my motorcycle out of the muddy used-car lot and rode on north to Elmira New York. I got a motel there that had a pool where I could swim, take a hot shower and mellow out at their bar. A beer or two was enough. Since no one at the bar was noticing that I came by motorcycle—and I was too tired to broadcast an announcement about it, I forgot about the rainy unpleasantness of the trip so far and went to my room to try to assemble ideas on how to summarize the rest of the 43 years of experiences in hundreds of different locations. The most common theme in all these memories was obvious: It was and is that I've enjoyed life in the rural areas of the country. Let's take a minute to see what I mean by "country life."

THE AMISH PEOPLE
An Amish farmer.

In my simple minded view, the Amish communities represent the quintessence of country living, the most perfect manifestation of the qualities that fit my definition of "country life." With almost no interest in or regard for institutional structures, they live closer than most people to a primitive or barter based society, in a

---

1.   Later, to revise and correct my memories, I used motel and campground receipts, charge card and check book records and the trip reports I sent to my family after most trips.

regime that you might say occupies a delicate balance point between the totally primitive, the loin cloth and spear cultures—and the totally modern highly structured societies.

Of course "country life" can be defined in endless ways and I don't mean to include what Rousseau called the completely "unmediated life." Even the Amish people live with a set of shared principles that lend a degree of structure to their communities. Specifically, they share what you might call a New Testament value system with regard to interpersonal matters, e.g. "Do unto others as you would have them do unto you…etc." But they have a very minimal interest in the kind of job specialization that leads to the efficiencies of more "highly developed" cultures, i.e. "urban life."

By now it's obvious that I am attracted to a form of "Country Life," as long as it's not completely devoid of such modern conveniences as motorcycles, hot water and bar food. My comments above about the Amish culture just provide a reference point to help me describe how what I have seen of life "in the country" differs from the urban or city life that most of us have lived.

The Country Life I have observed is a bit more sophisticated than the Amish model, but reflects many of the same principles. There is still the minimal interest or involvement with hierarchic considerations, little interest in national affairs or governmental developments, and very little interest in developing modern specialized skills.

I've only had one conversation with an Amish man. The Amish settlements closest to where I live are just east of Lancaster, Pennsylvania. I've passed through the area on many of my motorcycle trips north from Virginia and have always looked for opportunities to make personal contact with some Amish people. It's a treat to talk with the Amish ladies in the Lancaster Marketplace and I have tried everything the Pennsylvania Tourist organizations have to offer. In 2002 I finally got to have a real conversation with an Amish farmer—one of those who have not changed his way of life to accommodate the mass of tourists that now invade the areas where he and his friends live.

On that day the summer sun had just begun to warm the fields and I was quite disconnected from any other aspects of "reality" as I rode my motorcycle slowly to enjoy the scenery on a beautiful two lane country road out of Lancaster that I began to feel had been put there many years ago, just for me and an occasional Amish wagon. A tunnel of trees enclosed me on my private road as I drifted quietly along in a sort of peaceful trance, subconsciously headed for a campground near White Horse. I think it was on route 340. I slowly focused on some movement ahead of me on the left. It was as an Amish farmer leading two enormous horses out of his barn, which opened toward the road I was on. I was on my very quiet BMW, but I shut off my engine and coasted to a stop where his dirt driveway met my black top road. He paused on his driveway at the road edge across from where I had parked on the shoulder, and waited for me to speak.

I said good morning as I dismounted and explained that I had stopped to avoid frightening his magnificent horses, although we both knew this was just a tactic being used to start a conversation. The big horses stood so quietly that I wondered if they too were Amish. He stood between them with one hand on each halter, his beard, baggy trousers, wide suspenders and straw hat identifying him as Amish—and smiled as he said some strange version of "Thank you friend."

I made some awkward and nonsensical, comment about having seen many of the Amish wagons pulled by beautiful trotters, but it was unusual to see such magnificent draft horses so close to a public road. He let the halters drop as (I think) he said they were Belgians. He then removed his hat to wipe the sweat from his forehead with a large colored handkerchief, and it made me feel that he wasn't anxious to get rid of me. I felt a bit tongue-tied after my lame excuse for stopping, but recovered somewhat when he offered that he was just taking the horses across the road into one of his fields.

He showed no curiosity about me, my motorcycle or why I was on this road. For each of my cautious questions, he would pause as if he didn't hear, and then answered slowly, in simple and straightforward but minimal terms. I can't remember just what we talked about but I remember that he asked me no questions so I couldn't get family or travel stories going. I knew something of the Amish views on insurance, education, military service, social security and so forth and went on clumsily trying to expand our "conversation." Maybe he just wanted to please me when I finally went almost completely dumb and mentioned something about how difficult it must be for those without electricity. He finally responded with more than a minimum comment. He pointed to a small water wheel about 50 yards away in the stream by his barn. It was obviously very old, about a yard in diameter with paddles about a foot-wide.

He left the horses standing and we walked over to the water wheel. He was very proud of it. His grandfather had built it. The wheel moved a vertical rod up and down. The top of the rod pulled and released tension on a flexible wire that ran up and over a pulley and suspended on poles went on to his house, where he said it pumped water from his well. I could only imagine how it worked at the other end, but he made an effort to explain it by making a circular motion with one hand and an up-and-down motion with the other (like the drive shafts between the big wheels of a locomotive).

He seemed genuinely friendly, never impatient with me, and, much as I hated to end our conversation, I couldn't think of a way to keep it going after he showed me the wheel. I thanked him for the friendly visit and he shook my hand with a firm grip.

This brief visit confirmed what I had read of these people; not interested in material things, current events, or structured social programs—a minority group that does not ask for anything from those outside their community, and are seemingly uninterested in national or world affairs. They do sell farm products in the local markets but do not center their social life in towns. We've all read of their cooperative efforts in building homes and barns, and their weekly and seasonal get-togethers, but one wonders about the effects of their minimal communications.

SMALL TOWNS
Many small town bartenders.

Life in the typical small towns that I like to camp near is not as primordial as life in Amish country, but it is still almost as different from life in the cities and cosmopolitan areas of the country as the Amish areas are. I'm talking about towns of a few hundred people, almost all of whom know each other quite intimately.

In general, these towns have no nearby shopping centers, movies, motels or restaurants. In these, the daily social life is often limited to church, firehouse activities or dialog in a local bar.

As mentioned earlier, my yearly trips have been heavily flavored with conversations in roadside and small town bars. In the 1950s I lived in a town of about 300, called Stittville, about 20 miles outside of Rome, N.Y. I was a volunteer fireman for seven years there and active in the Methodist Church—as well as the local "Melrose" bar.

I have since visited so many of these country bars that I think I am qualified to make a few general observations about them. We'll talk about the ones in small towns first and then about two other types later.

Of course almost all bars have the standard neon beer-brand signs supplied by the Beer Companies, but in small towns the socializing is entirely different from other bars. To start with, everybody knows everybody. I'm talking about towns that are little more than a crossroads—where the population isn't large enough to support its own Moose, Elk or Masonic Lodge.

Of the few choices for social interaction, the bar provides the least "structured" option. It's the only choice open to both men and women almost every evening with no "membership" considerations like the firehouse and church have. The bar welcomes everyone. Of course the beer, liquor and bar food are factors, but they are not the only attractions. These people like to socialize.

Using some convenient generalizations let me try to develop a realistic description of life in these bars.

In villages of less than a few hundred residents, I have usually found from three to seven "regulars" in the bars when I arrive around early dinner time. As others arrive, everyone, including the bar tender, is greeted by first name. As soon as they are seated, these folks query each other regarding who of the regulars is missing. Then they talk about the missing ones.

They all seem to know everything about each other and about everyone else in the town, going back a generation or two. ("Yeah. Harry's just like his father when it comes to women…") During this reviewing and "refreshing" of the slowly changing town gossip, a few of the men check the always present TV set blaring down over the bar and branch off into comments on last week's and next week's sports events. They've seen my motorcycle as they came in and it's about at this stage that someone, bored with the usual dialog, starts a conversation with me. More on that in a minute.

In these rural areas, roughly a third of the patrons are construction workers, county employed road workers or farm hands. (Farm *owners* eat at home.) These guys who work out-of-doors tend to arrive around five o'clock. A few "trades" people from auto-body shops, a nearby gas station, or a co-op store, arrive around six.

Naturally everyone at these bars becomes curious when anything new gets on their agenda, like when a stranger arrives on a motorcycle.

"That your motorcycle outside?"

"Yep".

"You from Virginia?"

"Yes"

"Where yuh' headed?"

"Just touring the country"—

This launches a few questions and then develops into either of two themes for the next hour's dialog. One is some variation on the "I wish I could do that" theme. The other is about the Harley or Indian motorcycle that someone in the family has, or used to have, and usually about the tragic consequences. I can usually transition this theme into a couple of my "adventures" stories.

If there's a woman present, it isn't long before she squeezes in some personal questions about my family, their feelings about my travels and whether my wife ever rides with me.

I usually spring for a round of drinks for those who are conversing with me. This tends to promote at least a touch of camaraderie and from there things can go anywhere. In Chapter One, I mentioned how discussions in a bar got me a couple of my "one-day-jobs." In another it led to a night in a teepee. And there was the happy hour with the Métis man in Saskatoon.

One variation has to be considered a member of this small town model. That's the "neighborhood" bar. There are hundreds of neighborhood bars along the route of the Erie Canal in upstate, New York. The New York Central Railroad follows this route from NYC to Buffalo and on out to Chicago. The route passes many towns and villages where various ethnic groups, mostly Catholic, settled in the days when the Erie Canal was dug. Over the years, Friday night has become a Fish Fry night in these towns. The RR used to drop off fresh fish from the Fulton Fish Market New York City to all of these towns. So the smaller towns that are within about 15 miles either side of the rail line empty out on Friday nights as their population used to cluster into the "Fish Fry" locations along the rail line.

Fish Fry dinners are not expensive and a lot of beer is consumed-also at low prices. Utica Club, Genesee and Matt's Premium are popular brands in the towns I'm most familiar with in upstate New York.

The men who work in the "trades" or in construction usually leave early for home to get their scolding for "hanging out in bars" and holding up dinner. They've usually had three to five beers and sometimes a couple of greenish eggs—with salt—and possibly some pickled pig's feet, from the cloudy jar with the greenish rings around its inside. This group is easy to make friends with. They deal in simple good humor.

For this group I occasionally squirm a little on the bar seat when I first arrive and explain to the nearest guy how my legs are stuck in a bow-legs position from all day on the road and how I would have appreciated some help getting me off the beast, into the bar and onto a bar stool. Most people have felt just enough of this "crippling" experience as they get out of a car after a few hours of driving to give me some good humored sympathy.

Departures of the early group of beer drinkers begins at about six o'clock when the folks who work eight to five start to arrive; people from local shops, county employees and guys who are coming home from jobs in larger towns nearby. The first whiskey drinks begin at this time. These bring in jokes, comments on the news and some degree of "outsider" behavior, e.g. they don't know quite as much about the other local people as the earlier people did.

At around seven, a few local wives often join their husbands for a few beers and conversation with everyone—not just with the other women. Throughout the evening the first name intimacy continues and elements of the behavior of every group contribute to the atmosphere that follows throughout the evening and into the night.

On nights when I'm tenting, my last drink is sometimes a boiler maker—to protect me from whatever snakes or people might bite me during the night. It also serves as a ritualized way of saying "this is my last" before someone else sets up another round.

Very little of what I've said about bars in these very small towns is true for city bars or bars at resorts. In city bars, one is usually limited to conversations with people or couples on either side of you. They still have the need to talk, but don't know the others around the bar, much less their circumstances or any gossip of mutual interest. And for some reason they tend to present an ego-stimulated false persona. The third category of bars is what I call the Resort Bars. We'll talk about Resort Bars when we get to the Elkins Bar in Chapter Six.

But first—Did I tell you about the woman who undressed for me?

THE STRIPPER
A lady with a rash.

It was a very hot day on a country road leading me north toward Roaring Springs, Pennsylvania. The heat from the blacktop mixed with that from the hot engine under my saddle made sweat run down my face and neck from under my helmet. Please forget for the moment some of what I said in the Introduction about how good it feels to go out into the fresh "unprocessed" air. I was damned hot and pulled into an old roadside bar that sat all by itself somewhere around 20 miles south of Roaring Springs.

There were three local men at one end of the bar and a very heavy lady, who I sat down next to, seated around the middle of the bar. After the "where yuh headed" routine and her telling me how her son was severely hurt in a motorcycle accident, (Theme II described earlier.) I ordered a round of beers for the five of us. It was obvious that they had all been in the bar for quite a while.

As the lady sipped her suds, she felt obliged to explain to me that she was really in the bar because she had a severe heat rash and on very hot days she needed to be in an air-conditioned place. This explanation caused her three "friends" down at the end of the bar to snicker and mumble things about "it seems to be a year round problem." She was embarrassed and I wanted to move on anyway, so I finished my glass and started to get off the bar stool. At this, the lady got off her stool, turned her back toward me, and pulled her flimsy house dress up over her head to show me a severe rash on her back! I said something about how painful it looked and left with the bartender smiling and the three other guys now chuckling and mumbling something like "there she goes again."

SWIMMING HOLES
Lots of kids.

We can't leave the small towns without talking about swimming. Since I usually travel in the hottest part of summer, I'm almost always looking for places to swim. And since I try to travel rural or country roads, it some-times takes a bit of effort to locate the local swimming places.

I've mentioned that I stop to ask any kids I find along the roads. Unlike many city kids, they are. without exception, always helpful. Maybe it's because country folks like motorcycles and don't associate them with criminal behavior. Kids are my best source,—always happy to show me where they swim, where it's safe to dive or jump off the bridge—or swing out over the water on the Tarzan rope.

For my trip in 2001, I found a website called Swimming Holes East at " swimmingholes.org" on the web. The site identifies "moving fresh water spots such as in creeks, rivers, springs and waterfalls" and some "unique lakes, quarries and bays." It's a wonderful site. I reported my roughly planned route and it pro-vided a dozen maps with accompanying pictures of places that I then visited on the trip. In each of these spots I enjoyed a swim—mostly with youngsters, and all of them were memorable.

(When you see my clothes on the bike and my shoes on the ground,—that usually means I'm swimming nearby.)

I have a few favorite swimming holes that I have gone back to several times over the years. Their locations aren't important to my story, but I'd like to mention a few. My personal favorite is the branch of the Delaware River on the edge of my parent's farm near Andes, N.Y.—a place called "The Hook." The river is too shallow there to interest anyone other than a trout fisherman, but my family has fond memories of happy times there. Each summer we would dig the creek stones out of an area in the river and pack them to make a dam, just downstream from where we dug. The result was a shallow "swimming pool" about three feet deep where we could sit for hours in the water and continue to dig up stones to patch the ever leaking dam. Now I just like to sit in or by it for a few minutes when I'm near the place. In fact, one of my daughters was up to an affair on the Hook this summer. During the day, she slipped away from the group and went through the woods to bath in the nude at our old "swimming hole." It felt good for me to see that I've passed some such sentiments along to my children.

Another favorite of mine is in a cold stream about three miles west of Oliverea, N.Y. (stop at telephone pole marked 167.5.) When my kids were young it used to be called "Crazy Nellie Falls," because a lady had drowned herself there many years ago. Now the State has named it "Otter Falls." Before I rode motorcycles, my family visited my in-laws in Big Indian quite often. From Big Indian we could walk to Crazy Nellie—but more often we would just swim where the same stream passed under a railroad trestle closer to their home—where it, the stream, passed right by my father-in-law's house.

I often stop at Big Indian on my motorcycle trips, on my way to or from "The Hook." I stop the motorcycle on a small bridge that overlooks where we used to "swim" in knee deep water. From the bridge, the stream looks too shallow to ever have been such a fun place.

You should know that I am one of the fortunate souls who have a home on a lake. I live on Lake of the Woods, near Fredericksburg, Virginia. And my children grew up while living in a lakeside home on Lake Delta, near Rome, New York. So needless to say, we are a family of swimmers.

4

SOME PIECES OF NEW YORK AND PENNSYLVANIA

MY HOME TOWN
Some old friends remodeled.

While visiting some dozens of swimming holes in the north east, I became aware of how much the communities along them have changed over the years. It gave me a melancholy feeling, a sort of variation on the feeling of homesickness that borders on a hunger, for things or places associated with the past.

At the turn of the century, in 2000, I decided to motorcycle up to my old home town near the George Washington Bridge to Manhattan. I figured I would drift on north from there along the Hudson River to visit West Point and the old Roosevelt and Vanderbilt mansions on the other side of the river.

Englewood was a small village when I lived there from 1924 until WWII. Wealthy people, many of whom worked in N.Y.C., lived on "The Hill" near where Englewood Cliffs overlooks Manhattan. Their maids, chauffeurs, landscapers, butchers, bakers and barbers lived down the "seven sisters" yellow brick road called Palisade Avenue, around the town's RR Tracks. A predominately black neighborhood, unofficially called "Texas," was located even further from the Hill.

My dad was a chauffeur and mom was a maid until she "retired" to raise four kids. I took a ride around all three of the old three regions. I then parked the motorcycle on Bergen Street, which is a half mile from the good side of the tracks, where I lived in my early school years. Nothing seemed the same. All distances are now shorter. All buildings have been replaced. Our house had been replaced by a telephone company parking lot. Our grade school, Franklin Elementary, has been replaced by a furniture store and Officer Beaman, who held up traffic so we could cross Engle Street to get to school, was nowhere to be seen…Office buildings have been built on the ball field that was behind the school. Several very chick small stores had replaced my Dad's old fashioned hardware store. The Mary Elizabeth restaurant where I worked all through High School had become a furniture store. St. Paul's Church, where I was a bell ringer, sang in the boy's choir and worked my way up to "Patrol Leader" of the "Moose Patrol" in good old Boy Scout Troop 22, has had much of its insides partitioned into offices.

During a brief chat with the current minister at St. Paul's about how things used to be, I spotted and pointed out to him a wood bench left from the twenty or so that we, the boys choir, used to sit on during the choir rehearsals three times a week some seventy years ago. I interpreted for him some of the initials we had carved on the backs of the benches. He seemed to be interested to hear about the bench's history and promised it would be kept as long as he was there.

Lonesome for evidence that I was really in the town of my youth, I called an old High School friend, Sam, who lived nearby in Hackensack. We'll hear about Sam in Chapter 6, but on this visit he was in poor shape; heart, lungs, joints, teeth, attitude—all worn out or replaced with a variety of plastic inserts, drainage tubes, valves and pills. We enjoyed looking through his old photo albums, and remembering the High School girls we both loved, but never had the courage to ask for a date and the lonesome waitresses we worked with in the Mary Elizabeth. We both reviewed our stories of our WWII experiences and the many times we had motorcycled together. His old motorcycle stood sadly in a corner of his garage, all covered with dirt it had gathered many years before.

My boyhood "Home Town" had become a foreign place. It was probably a mistake to go back and be forced to modify my highly tuned and well established memories of it.

WEST POINT AND THE HUDSON INSTITUTE

West Point is about an hour up-river from Englewood. Visitors are no longer allowed to ride around its grounds like we used to. They now have a fancy Visitors Center near the entrance with a history of the place and I took the bus tour they now offer from there to see that nothing much has changed there. After the tour I rode a few miles back south to cross the Bear Mountain Bridge and then headed north to visit the Roosevelt mansion.

Traveling on up the Hudson, I stopped at an old tavern in Rhinebeck called "Beekman Arms" to refresh some memories. I had made an earlier visit to see a flying club exhibit of old airplanes and talk to the guys who restored them and now show them off in occasional air shows.

I then went on up to visit old friends on the campus of "The Hudson Institute" where I had worked a few times on projects with futurist "Herman Kahn on ways to speed passenger transportation systems in President Kennedy's "Northeast Corridor" program. Older readers may remember Kahn's forecast book called "The Year 2000."[1] (the pill, the pot, the price of labor, the decline of family values, the resurrection of Japan, etc.)

Although these last few days were enjoyable as typical tourist trip stops, I can't say that I found opportunities to get acquainted with a variety of people. I find it strange that the denser the population the harder it is to make new friendships. I think it was Alvin Toffler who suggested (my personal interpretation) that the complexities of modern living cause us to compartmentalize our personalities so that we can deal with things or situations using an appropriate set of views, attitudes and behaviors that we needn't exercise under different sets of circumstances.[2] I think this "compartmentalizing" sublimates a major portion of what people really think or are willing to reveal to others, i.e. don't reveal one's "real" self. But I must admit that being comfortable in several different compartments is really the definition of sophistication. I feel that the phenomenon is especially vivid in the business climate of the northeast corridor and its immediate environs—where I worked all my life—and it wasn't until I turned west at Albany and north on what's called the Thruway Extension to Lake George, that I felt I was getting away from it and closer to "real" (whole) people

I was headed for "The Year 2000 Americade Motorcycle Rally" in the town of Lake George New York.

A MOTORCYCLE RALLY
Lots of bikers

You might be surprised to hear that a motorcycle rally has some of the characteristics of the small town bar scene. Attendees make a concerted effort to be sociable. After all, for most of them it's their once a year motorcycle trip away from home. They, like me, use their bikes and their trip stories as a basis for communication.

---

1.   Kahn, Herman & Wiener, Anthony. *The Year 2000*...MACMILLAN Co.,N.Y.
2.   Toffler, Alvin. *The Third Wave*. Bantom Books, N.Y.

There's really only one significant street in Lake George. It parallels the lake shore and was packed tight with footpeg-to-footpeg motorcycles, parked on both sides. Creeping bikes, three or four abreast, with leather clad riders crowded the space between the rows of parked bikes and flowed, as a glued—together mass, slowly down the center of the street. One by one they peeled off to park their bikes, snap open a can of beer and start a conversation with other bikers. (This would be in the "biker" compartment, of my theory of multiple personality packages mentioned earlier) but most bikers have no other compartments.) Some would then head for a swim at the beach just a block away and parallel to the main drag.

It was fun kidding with the crowd and looking over the fascinating array of motorcycles and the scantily clad women…Everyone was reasonably well behaved, although there were some crazy antics in the lake by a few who needed to "fondle" their women more than was acceptable at street side. The prices for beer had been doubled, but nobody seemed to mind. Booze didn't make an appearance until late in the evening when everyone seemed to need a little stimulation, having sat on their machines most of the day drinking beer. The police tried to make friends with everyone and handled minor incidents with tact and flexible interpretations of rules.

In the early evening I was swapping motorcycle stories with a couple of Harley riders in their motel room when they decided to start riding home that night to beat the rain being forecast on TV for the next few days. I didn't look forward to going back to my tent, so I made a deal with them to take over their air-conditioned motel room and enjoyed the evening talking with a few people who liked air conditioning more than sweating on a motorcycle seat.

The following morning brought rain as predicted. I was glad I hadn't tried to sleep in the tent. The planned Rally program of outdoor activities didn't seem very appealing in the rain, so after breakfast I went back from downtown Lake George to the campgrounds to pick up my wet tent. I then headed south through Saratoga Springs and rode a couple of hundred miles toward Andes, N.Y. where I have spent many evenings in the bar of the old Andes Hotel

THE CATSKILLS—BEAR STORIES AND ANDES
Bear hunters

The rain continued with me again on the way south from Lake George. It was so bad that I pulled into an office driveway where the front entrance to the building had an overhang. I went into the lobby and asked to use the bathroom, but the guard wouldn't let me pass his desk. I stood in the lobby for a few minutes and decided I had to move on. I hadn't had any breakfast at the wet campground—not even coffee. So when I stopped for gas, I was pleased to find some food and rest from the tension of riding on the slippery blacktop roads.

The gas station had a deli case with a sandwich bar—and a few tables and chairs. I wound up spending an hour there with some local Adirondack characters who, although they were traveling by pickup truck, were also taking cover from the rain. I bought and shared with them a half-pound of liverwurst, an onion, a bag of rolls and a couple of tear-to-open mustard things I had acquired at a McDonalds. They bought the sodas and we talked.

My friends were hunters—bear hunters. Between liverwurst sandwiches, I heard a lot of folklore about the differences between Grizzly bears and Black bears. Some of what they told me I had read in a book about the Appalachian Trail, but my friends gave the impression that their wisdom came from personal experience.[3] I now know how the Black bears seem to grin before they eat you if you made them run to catch you, and how they climb trees to eat your legs before they break the branches that you tied your food to so they wouldn't get it. And I also know that Grizzlies like to come into your tent and eat your arms and chew on your lips when you haven't washed all the odor of dinner away adequately before retiring.

Since I camp out a lot, I vowed to never eat again without disposable gloves on.

The Andes Hotel let me put my motorcycle and wet luggage in a barn behind the Hotel. I pulled out some dry clothes, took a shower and called my cousins, Ethel and Bob Reynolds, whose families have been farmers just off "Bullet Hole Road" in Andes for several generations. In a pattern we have established over 40 years, they joined me for dinner at the old hotel and I joined them for breakfast the next day at their farm. We did our annual tour of the old barn with its three tractors, (one working) their home-built saw mill, their homemade log splitter, two old motorcycles—a BMW and a Norton—and other miscellaneous machinery. I visited their son Wayne and his wife Alma in the house they built on their parent's farm. Their brother, John, also built a home on the farm. Both used lumber they had cut from the family property and sawed into planks in their own saw mill. Such planks are of differing widths and are used in floors and overlapping planks as part of outside walls of colonial houses. Here's something you may have already guessed. The board widths varied because as trees were cut length-

---

3.   Bryson, Bill…*A walk in the Woods.* Broadway Books, 1998, N.Y.

wise to make planks, the width of the planks varied from wide center cuts to narrower planks from near the outer circumference of the tree.

As I went to bed after a fun evening, I once again had to murmur thanks to the Lord that down to earth people like these could still be found, people with only one persona, un-interested in credentials, rank, titles or even in competition. What you see is what is real. These are people unencumbered by any need to craft an artificial persona. There is little time spent talking about the larger issues of the nation or international affairs. It's enough to deal with those of the town and the family.

Climbing the mountains on a chilly morning as I headed south, I had to stop twice for small groups of deer standing in the road ahead of me. I stopped to take pictures. Near the second stop I saw a lonely looking restaurant that looked like a cabin. I went in for pancakes. The place was empty. The couple that owned it had recently retired from NYC. The three of us sat together as they served my breakfast and queried me about my travels. They said they had sufficient retirement income to "do our own thing," which was to have a place like this in the mountains—even if it didn't make money. They said they loved it, but admitted they were a bit lonesome. (It was about eight a.m. and I hadn't seen a vehicle on the road since I left Andes an hour earlier.)

As I left them wiping the table where we ate together, I had a feeling that they felt they had made a mistake undertaking such a radical change. I made a pledge to myself—to come back in a year and see how they were doing.

Let's go back now to the rainy road to Cazenovia in Chapter 3.

OLD CARS IN CAZENOVIA
A pretty bank cashier and some old people who love old cars

You may recall that it was raining when I ducked into an empty car in a used car lot. I left the car when the rain seemed to have stopped, but it started again. After a night's rest in an Elmira motel, it still rained and I pulled under cover at a bank cashier's car service window, to put my rain suit back on.

I tried to keep the bank cashier chatting with me through her window as the occasional cars came in to use the other bank lanes to conduct their transactions with a second cashier. After a few semi-humorous remarks about my wetness and my much loved old sneakers, I still needed more time. So I asked her to tell me the route to Cazenovia, and then to give me more details about every turn along her suggested route. Her answers gave me some more time under cover. With good humor she cooperated with my stalling and answered me laughingly as she watched me pack my regular shoes and put on my old drive-in-the-rain sneakers and change into my completely ineffective "water resistant" jacket. We both tried to smile—me the pitiable, she the giver of pity, as I launched back into the rain and headed north.

About an hour after I left the lady at the bank window, I arrived in the beautiful town of Cazenovia N.Y. where I enjoy attending the annual Franklin Motorcar Club meeting. It's the same kind of club meeting that many owners of old cars or motorcycles arrange for a week in the summer, a gathering of old timers who enjoy swapping stories about their cars or motorcycles.

The Franklin Club arranges for its members to stay in Cazenovia State College dormitories for a few days every summer. It's a lot like an Elder Hostel. The car owners sit together amongst their cars on a green lawn surrounded by trees on the College campus. A few cars have their hoods up to help clarify some feature that came up in the conversations.

There is always an interest in how much modification has been made to a particular car. The "Purists" try to maintain all the "original equipment", but that usually means they have to trailer their cars to the meeting. Very few would chance driving their treasure on a modern highway. And "hand cranks" are too difficult for most ole timers to deal with. Townspeople wander around to see the cars, but surprisingly few. The town seems to enjoy having the club there each year, mostly I think because of the business they bring in. But it could be based on the camaraderie that had expanded from what the members had to include the folks who visited with them every year while they were housed on the campus. Franklins were, and still are, very unique cars in that they have air-cooled engines; no radiators, no water pumps and no hoses. When I got out of the Navy in 1946, I bought a 1929 Franklin coupe from a junk yard. My sisters and I were the only people who thought it was beautiful. It had blue leather upholstery and a rumble seat. In college, where everyone wanted a new car, it made me something of a campus oddity and I got a good deal of experience fixing and replacing most of its parts. That experience now qualifies me to sit all day and talk with a friendly bunch of old Franklin owners.

A favorite observation that the club members bring up every year is how, in the old days, gas station attendants used to check the water in car radiators. Since the Franklin had no radiator, they would try in vain to twist the hood ornament off. Simply repeating stories about this seems to provide sufficient incentive for members to return each year to tell them again.

In the dozen or so years that I made it to these club meetings, I've always enjoyed sitting, surrounded by the great old cars, and in the shade of the great old campus trees, chatting with the great old Franklin lovers. We would usually speculate on how much my experience with air-cooled engines might have stimulated my interest in motorcycles. Being people who love engines of any kind, they always admired my air-cooled BMW. But since I now have a four-cylinder water-cooled motorcycle engine, I have to argue with the old Franklin Club members.

I argue that water cooling allows tighter tolerances within the engine, more compact designs that do not require cooling fins—and quieter engines due to the water jacket effect. The members claimed that technical people have no sense of romance and I am considered a sort of traitor because I once owned, but had abandoned, an air cooled motorcar and now had abandoned an air cooled motorcycle. Nevertheless, they always encourage me to "return next year" and again repeat or repent my views.

At these annual gatherings, lots of people pay to get a ride around the Cazenovia countryside in a parade of old Franklins, and the whole town enjoys seeing and hearing them rumble down the road, so majestic and proud of themselves.

THE ONEIDA EXPERIMENT

I enjoy talking about cars and motorcycles, but I have to admit that I've talked to these same people many times on my annual trips. Now I'm off from Cazenovia for a beautiful country ride east to Oneida, New York.

My wife likes it when I visit Oneida. That's where the Oneida Silver Company sells "seconds" of all their silver products. I call and tell her what is on special sale and mail home what I can't strap on the bike.

The history of the Oneida Community is another fascinating diversion for a curious guy who only intended to stop for coffee. According to their tourist pamphlets, Oneida was "the most extreme form of communistic experiment ever established in the U.S." What always interested me were the details of how they implemented their belief that everyone shares everything in the community. All the women belonged to all the men. The older men could each choose a young virgin for "training" but she would not be restricted from "training" with any other man who wanted to "help out" (with the training). They practiced some fascinating sex stuff that the Visitors Center won't discuss, but they will tell you what web site to check. Life was complicated for the men: ("Good night, Honey. I've got to get over to Betty and Joan's house. See you on Thursday.")

I have to presume that the best looking women produced the children and the other women raised them. But nobody I met in the town wanted to discuss it. All they cared about was the "good deal" one could get at the Oneida Silver factory.

So I rode on to Rome, New York, where there are some Italians who will discuss anything that has to do with good looking women.

ROME, NEW YORK

After a few days of eating meals with strangers, it was a nice break to join an old friend in a bar and restaurant where we had spent a lot of time together 45 years ago. I had called ahead to make the date with Fred as soon as I knew when my wanderings would enable a stop in Rome. When I arrived, I proceeded as usual, borrowing the Yellow Pages at the Food Lion store to use with my cell phone to survey the motel availability and prices.

It was a warm July afternoon, so after unloading my still-wet gear at the Green Lantern motel, I put on my bathing trunks and cycled a couple of miles in a light drizzle for a swim in Lake Delta. There I wanted to see a house on the lake where I once lived and raised four children.

Lake Delta dams the Mohawk River to hold the water needed to maintain an appropriate level in the Erie Canal—the canal later re-named the "Barge Canal."

BAPTIZING THE MINISTER
A minister and some firemen

I used to paddle my kids and houseguests from below the Lake Delta dam to pass the Fish Hatchery and the Air Force Base, and paddle on down stream about seven miles on the Mohawk River, into the city of Rome. There my wife would pick us up behind The Savoy bar with our car, which had racks for a canoe on its roof. The river ride got so popular that lots of friends from the area would ask to take it. But the rides all ended one cold day in the fall of 1958 when Rome's Newspaper Headlines reported that Rev. Mitchell, beloved minister of the Rome Methodist Church, was in the Rome Hospital with pneumonia, having barely escaped drowning in a canoe accident on the icy Mohawk River. Seems he was canoeing with winter clothes on, with a deacon from his church, one William Mason, when they rounded a bend in the river to face a fallen tree blocking their passage. The canoe hit the tree, swung sideways into its branches and filled with the river's rushing cold water. Both canoers wound up in the river.

The Newspaper went on to report that the rushing water kept the Rev. Mitchell more-or-less stuck in the water-filled canoe jammed into the tree's branches. Mason, who had dressed lightly, managed to work his way under the canoe and underwater through the tree's branches, to scramble ashore downstream. He then climbed out on the fallen tree to pull the hysterical Minister, who was loaded in heavy and wet clothing, up through the branches and onto the tree trunk where he clung shivering and unable to move, much less crawl, toward shore. Mr. Mason, unable to move him, promised him he wouldn't report things the minister had muttered, and ran through the woods to the nearby Lake Delta Firehouse from which he brought back several volunteer firemen to help get Rev. Mitchell unlocked from the tree and safely ashore. He had been severely chilled and was diagnosed as having pneumonia. The newspaper asked that "Get Well" cards and letters be sent to room xxx at Rome Hospital or to the Rome Methodist Church.

Rev. Mitchell recovered—at least physically. But just as Deacon Mason's adult bible class would never again get into a lesson unless he repeated the story first, Rev. Mitchell never got over imagining he heard people whispering about God's purpose in granting him this wonderful "river adventure."

My aluminum canoe was winched out of the tree by the Fire Department guys, but it had what is called a broken back which I was never able to repair.

Now, 45 years later, I parked my motorcycle in front of the lake house I used to live in and enjoyed a swim and a walk around my old house. I didn't see the current residents to ask for an inside house tour and whether the water stain on the living room ceiling had bled through the fresh paint job I had done so long ago. (I had hammered a nail through a hidden water pipe while flooring for the new bedrooms I was adding upstairs.)

I explained to my ever patient and faithful motorcycle why I was pausing at this location as I returned to the Green Lantern Motel to take a shower, shave, and find my way to the Savoy Bar and Grill in "downtown" Rome, I rode through the Air Force Base that, in the 1950s used to be the major employer in the town.

At the Savoy I found my old friend, Fred, one martini ahead of me.

We did a lot of remembering together. In the 1950s this bar had hummed with Company Representatives—who came to Rome almost weekly to try for early information on Air Force procurements being organized by the Rome Air Development Center and electronic equipment procurements from a division of the Air Materiel Command at Rome's Griffiss Air Force Base. The base has long since closed. My ride through the quiet, lonesome buildings, now used mainly as commercial warehouses, was very depressing—Once again I got the "you can't go home" feeling.

Fred and I talked about our kids, mutual friends who once populated the Savoy and some of our joint adventures of long ago. It was a long night. You know how old men are once they've had a few martinis and start talking about the good old days.

Due to the radical change in the clientele at The Savoy Bar after the Air Force Base closed, the bar doesn't fit neatly into the list of three bar types that I discussed in Chapters Three and Five.

In its prime, The Savoy was a variation on the Type Three, the Resort kind of bar. The many Company Representatives who inhabited the Savoy in the 1950s came into town for a few days every week or two. Unlike conventional vacationers at resorts, they did get to know one another in a kind of shallow golf partner way. Not much was said about wives and children or local gossip, but friendships were formed. Expense account money doesn't generate the kind of neighborly or community relationships one finds in small town bars. But neither does it settle for impersonal discussions. Setting schedules for golf games is about the level of intimacy found here.

With the closing of the Air Base and the end of the military procurements that were once conducted there, the Savoy is quieter now. Local people have replaced the Company Reps. Less money is thrown around and it's a peaceful place for old timers like Fred and me to reminisce about "the good old days."

A REALLY BAD DAY

This morning, when I was partially recovered from my evening at the Savoy, I looked out of my window in the Green Lantern Motel to see if my motorcycle was still there, it was overcast, but not raining. So I checked out of the motel at about seven A.M. and started for Syracuse where I had attended a doctorate program in the '50's. A light rain, accompanied by thunder and lightning, started when I was about 10 miles from the motel. I mumbled "Dammit!" or something like that, and U-turned to race back to the motel to get some coffee and to drip dry before the motel's check out time.

Crashes of lightning stimulated me to hurry, and the wind, from looking back over my shoulder while passing a car, tore my glasses off. It took me a hundred yards on the wet pavement to cautiously get the machine stopped safely on the shoulder of the highway. Passing trucks sprayed water on me as I walked back along the highway to find the glasses. It seemed like it was going to be a bad day—maybe a record breaker. Maybe even worse than the one when I checked into a campground in Vermont, only to find that my tent pack had come loose from the motorcycle and blown off somewhere, leaving me with a couple of idle bungee cords and a picnic table for a bed and shelter.

After an hour of TV back at the motel, the storm had gone east and the sun began to creep out. But the day didn't get better. When back on Route 5 the sun finally dried my shirt.

But then cruising at about 60 mph, what I call a "type two" bug hit me.

BAD BUGS

I've studied bugs ever since I took up motorcycling. A "Type One" bug is the ordinary kind that flies around, carefree, and more-or-less out of control. It shocks both you and him or her self when it accidentally smacks into your face. It stings for a few seconds, but mostly just makes you wince (or, on *really bad* days, to spit it out). It's easy to forgive these kinds of bugs. They are dumb, but they mean no harm.

The "Type Two" bug is the nasty kind. These purposely carry some version of a "stinger" in their tail, usually filled with some kind of disgusting juice. They come toward you head-on, leisurely traveling at about 5 mph, with their little white teeth gleaming in a smile, even as they think about what's about to happen when they execute their magnificent stabbing maneuver. About a yard before they hit your face, they do a quick, and quite graceful, tummy-tuck, pulling up their knees to bring their rear end under and forward to harpoon you at 65 mph. (That's your 60 mph speed plus their 5 mph.) They prefer to hit near your sun glasses so one of your eyes will swell up for an hour or so and you can stay in a bad mood for another hour 'cause the edge of your glasses continues to jiggle against your face just enough to irritate the swollen brow. As I said, I got hit by a Type Two. (Type Three enters the helmet and horses around for a while as you try to get the damned helmet off. Just as you get the strap loose, it lets loose its spear.)

I figured that if it was going to continue as a really bad day, I should start worrying about what might happen next. My luggage was all on tight. It might be a flat tire or my drive shaft coming uncoupled between the motor and the rear wheels. But both of these things were already part of my experience, so it would probably be some new challenge. I guessed it was best to just slow down and be watchful. And try to think pleasant thoughts.

Having left Rome and now approaching Syracuse on route 5, with a swollen eye, and with the sun now shining into the other eye and the slit part of the wounded eye that was still open, I stopped to phone a professor who had been my Thesis Advisor at Syracuse University fifty years ago. It didn't occur to me that he, being older than I, would be dead by now. When I asked the secretary of the EE Department if he was around, she went into shock. She asked me when I had last talked to him. I sensed hostility and I said "Forgive me" and explained that I had a severe head wound from a Type 2 bug. This too seemed to disturb her. When she asked "Who the hell are you?" I hung up quickly and picked up my pace on route 5 west to get past Syracuse.

My "bad day" continued.

THE FINGER LAKES

If you look at a map, there are six long, side-by-side, lakes taking up space in central N.Y. (Don't look too close or you'll get seven.) All run north-south and on the map they look like fingers. They look like someone scratched them on the map with four finger nails and a thumb, (Oneida Lake). It's a beautiful region. No heavy industry. Just wineries and farms. Seneca Falls, Watkins Glen. Lots of towns with Indian names. I've enjoyed riding up and down the shores of these lakes many times and have had a dinner, boat ride and swim with a friend in Penn Yan on Keuka Lake at least a half dozen times.

There are Grape Vineyards on the Hills, interlaced with neat farm complexes—each with its own house, barn and one or two out buildings for farm equipment. On the land at the Lakes edge, small summer cottages and boat docks are snuggled together.

Did you ever notice that at the end of each row of grapes in a wine vineyard, there is a rose bush? I'm told that the color of the roses tells the winemaker how much acid is in the soil, so that he or she can add stuff to make it right. Check it out!

A BED IN A GARAGE
A lady in a B&B

One summer I was on the southern end of Keuka Lake in Hammondsport, N.Y., when it started to rain. It was late afternoon and I had been groping around for a place to stay. With no campsite in range, I said a brief prayer to Frigg (Goddess of the Skies—who also watches over home and marriage). She heard me and took emergency action because I soon spotted an open garage door by a tourist house. I pulled into the garage and sloshed over to the adjacent owner's house to ask the lady owner about a room. She was full, but said I could stay in her garage until the rain stopped We got chatting in her kitchen and Frigg told her to advise me that the rain wasn't going to stop (she must have heard my earlier prayer to Frigg)—She suggested that I pull out a cot that was stored in the garage, and stay the night in the garage. I accepted her offer—and was surprised to find that the cot had sheets on it!

While I was unstrapping stuff from the motorcycle, she came over to the garage with a sandwich of some sort and took a folding chair down from the wall to sit and talk with me. It turned out that she was a widow and operated her house as a Bed and Breakfast-and occasionally used the cot herself when she was able to rent her own bedroom! When I had arrived the B&B was full, but she didn't want me trudging in wet to use her room while she took the garage cot. She was lonesome and curious about my travels, so we chatted for an hour or so until she had to get back to other guests sitting in her living room.

In the morning I refreshed myself with a cold swim in Keuka Lake which was just across the street from the garage. I then found out that the cot rental included coffee, bacon and egg for breakfast.

A Canadian specialist in Yard Sales

I had another memorable experience that occurred due to a shower along a road through the Finger Lakes It was on a sunny day when I was cruising slowly on a smooth road and in spite of the beauty of the lake on one side of me and the farms and vineyards on the other, I got dangerously sleepy. When a light summer shower started I decided to pull into a motel. As I did, another motorcycle pulled in from the opposite direction and we met at the check-in desk.

I asked him if he would be interested in a swim in the rain by a bridge I had just crossed. (A small river ran into the lake near the motel.) He said no, but he would join me for a beer when I got back. So I picked up a six pack on my way back from the swim and we shared it after I showered.

He told me that he came down from Toronto to tour the summer yard sales in the lake regions. He said that local Finger Lakes residents gathered materials during the off-season for sale to the tourists who swarm around the lakes in the summer. The American dollar was worth $1.30 in Canadian money at that time and he said he had a source of U.S. dollars when he was here in the States, possibly from selling used stuff he brought down for U.S. yard sales. He said there were quotas on new goods crossing the border, but he told the customs people that the used stuff in his trailer was for personal camping, and not subject to duty. His big motorcycle had a trailer attached to carry his purchases. The funny part is that after we finished the six pack, he said he had some outside in his trailer. I watched from the door as he opened the trailer. It was full of what looked like old clothes!

I went to sleep trying to figure out what he was really up to. I decided to ask him over breakfast to go over how the exchange rate fit into his program, but in the morning he was gone.

THE GREAT LADY BIKER
Louise Sherbyn

Across the top ends of the "Finger Lakes," Route 5 runs east-west, more-or-less parallel to, the N.Y. barge canal.

Along route 5 and approaching the city of Waterloo, New York, there's a place where I once met a fascinating lady.

In 1972 I had read an article about Louise Sherbyn, a very attractive lady who used to ride a special all white Indian motorcycle with gold trim. Dressed in her snug fitting (in appropriate places) jodhpurs she posed for Indian sales promotions at county Fairs around the country in the late1930's when lady motorcyclists were somewhat rare. In the '50's she founded the Women's International Motorcycle Association.

LOUISE SHERBYN AND HER INDIAN

The magazine article said her home was in Waterloo, N.Y. I called her from Virginia while planning my 1974 trip and made a dinner date. That year was one of the few that I had a companion with me, a friend from work, Gene Rachialson. He too was fascinated with the magazine's description of this lady and asked if he could join me. After we got to the Waterloo Holiday Inn and changed clothes, I called Louise and she invited us for drinks at her house before going out to dinner.

Louise had set up a large pitcher of whiskey sours on a card table under a tree right next to the Seneca River, which ran along the rear boundary of her back yard.

She got out both of her magnificent white Indians. The older one had been shown in the magazine article I first read about her. We took pictures of me on her last one, which is now in the Indian museum. (The pictures here are old ones she gave me on a later visit.)

Louise told us wonderful stories of her adventures on trips around the country, in Canada and on a trip to Great Britain. Most of her travels were on dirt roads. One trip was to North Bay, Ontario, about 400 miles north of Toronto, to get her picture taken with the Dionne Quintuplets. (I later made that same trip. See Chapter Two) Most memorable were her news clippings of a horrifying story about a terrible experience she had. She was stopped by a log dropped as a roadblock on a dirt road near her home—and raped by four men, four brothers. They lived near the dirt road she often traveled coming home from the east. The clippings were about the incident and the subsequent trial. Law enforcement was very unorganized in those Bonnie and Clyde days, but Louise knew and was able to identify the men and where they lived. They all went to jail. But the regional reports of the crime made her a reputation as a "wild thing," running in a "man's world" of motorcyclists, while her husband preferred to stay on their farm. She felt that the criticisms isolated her from the social life in the small town, but that made her even more adventurous.

On my 1999 trip, twenty-five years after my first visit, I stopped in Waterloo to see her again. She was 96, deaf, nearly blind, and living in a nursing facility in Clifton Springs Hospital. I found her through the local police chief, Doyle Marquardt, who referred me to Louise's best friend, Stella Cornelius. Over dinner, Stella surprised me with the gift of an old cardboard box marked "for Bill Mason!" The box had about 400 pictures of Louise (two of which appear here) and other cyclists. Obviously we had bonded. The box had been in Stella's garage since Louise went into the nursing home. At that time she also gave the white Indian Sport that I had posed on for pictures, along with her collection of motorcycle toys, mostly cast iron models, to the Indian Motorcycle Museum in Springfield, Massachusetts.

That night, back at the Waterloo Holiday Inn, I removed the pictures from the very large old black albums, so I could carry them on the rest of my trip. I later gave some of them to a lady who wrote to me and said she wanted to incorporate them into a book, but I still have about 90 percent of them.

Louise had no children and her friend Stella was as old as Louise was. That Louise chose to leave her photos with me was very touching—and perhaps indicative of how isolated socially she was from the other residents of Waterloo. But I like to think that my thoughts on motorcycling were a bit odd, and very much like hers.

In October '03 my wife and I visited the Indian Motorcycle Museum in Springfield to see Louise's old white Indian Scout again, and read more about her in a special display they have there. I had seen a small display in the Waterloo Library's "Terwilliger Museum" on William Street, (not named after me), but no motorcycle. I tried to get some of the papers the local library collected from Louise's home, but they were sealed storage at the Terwilliger at that time.(2003) I still treasure the fascinating photos she left me and will continue to look a proper home for them.

HOW WE DUG THE ERIE CANAL

The place where we had our pitcher of Whiskey Sours by the Seneca River, behind Louise's house, was actually by a section of the Seneca River referred to as the Seneca Canal. The Seneca Canal connects two of the Finger Lakes, Cayuga and Seneca, and joins them to connect hundreds of New York farms to the great Erie Canal, now, since 1918, called the N.Y. State Barge Canal.

We, Louise, Gene and I, talked a lot about Canals. I, like Louise, lived for awhile on the Canal system; me in Rome, N.Y. on the Mohawk River which fed water to the canal and Louise here on the Seneca connector. As we talked, all three of us got to feeling mellow from the Whiskey Sours and the idea of the three of us with only a horse and some whiskey sours, digging a 400 mile ditch, 40 feet wide and four feet deep—with shovels,—from Albany NY to Buffalo, almost brought tears to our eyes as we competed to recall details of the effort and its effects. We got exhausted from shipping Midwestern farm produce east to the hungry Atlantic coast and carrying manufactured goods and immigrant labor west. It has never seemed as fantastic as it did that night. The fact that the barges only moved as fast as the mules could pull them was un-important compared to how much could be moved for the low cost of horse feed.

Digging the ditch provided the first employment for thousands of Italian, Polish, Irish and German immigrants who couldn't care less about what it would do for the country. Smaller groups of Hungarians, Russians and French also came. All of them eventually settled in communities along the canal where they retained the rites, rituals and special cooking techniques they brought from their home countries.

The cost of digging the canal was completely recovered in nine years by barge toll charges! By the time we finished the pitcher of sours, it seemed like the three of us might have personally dug the damned thing, and we were feeling proud of what we had done.

I had motorcycled along almost all of the Erie Canal in the 1980's. Actually I went from Amsterdam (near Albany) to Buffalo and Tonawanda, the real western terminal of the canal traffic. Tonawanda started as a shipping point for lumber, but with the two-way traffic between there and N.Y, it evolved a manufacturing orientation. I'd guess that the surplus labor available after the canal was completed was as important a factor in Tonawanda's development as a low cost transportation center. In any case, the town retained clusters or neighborhoods of families with the same ethnic backgrounds

That trip along the canal was a bit depressing one for me. I had known these towns in the 1950s when they were all fascinating stops along what were at the time country roads—places to visit on the special holidays associated with the ethnic population's culture. Life seemed less complex everyone enjoyed a sort of intimacy in their own sanctuary set in the pastoral beauty of the surrounding small farms, the nearby Great Lakes and the Adirondack Mountains.

My many conversations and observations during my travels tell me that things have not gotten better since those days when we thought that the new Thruway would connect us to each other and all of us to the Big Apple. All the Mills gradually moved to the south. The big Rome Cable and the Revere copper plants closed. Griffiss Air Force Base closed. In Buffalo and nearby Lackawanna, Bethlehem Steel, Ford, GM and Bell Helicopter closed or moved out. More than a dozen very old businesses moved out of, or died in, Tonawanda, the last real canal stop before Buffalo. Tonawanda had once been a focal point for feeding lumber and farm products by barge for transport to N.Y. City and bringing N.Y. stuff to the hinterlands. But as immigrants arrived to join families that had once worked on the canal, a large number of small manufacturing plants grew up there.

With all of these plant closures, thousands of people became unemployed and it greatly modified the comfortable life people once had in the towns along the great canal. Even the Thruway couldn't generate enough corporate investment to stop the out-migration. As those who lost jobs moved out, a different kind of people moved in and the entire social structure has now changed. The old neighborhoods where the Italian, Irish and German subgroups clustered and maintained their common cultural heritage, their languages, their wonderful foods, and their family orientation have been fractured by the invasion of people from other cultures who weren't part of the mass inflow of immigrants in the late 1800s, cultures that haven't yet coalesced from crowded households into neighborhood clusters like the earlier settlers did. The healthy work ethics that several foreign corporations have found attractive in Middle America are no longer present here—partially due to the welfare mentality that has developed after a generation of unemployment and I think partially to the "Death of God" syndrome that has modified people's views concerning ethics. "There's no sense looking for work when what there is pays less than my unemployment income."

The hollow feelings that I occasionally had as I talked with what is left of the neighborhoods in these towns is hard to describe. My conversations usually started with comments about the young people moving out, the influence of TV and movies and the better life kids become aware of in college. But I sense that the deeper feelings stem from a loss of heritage and tradition. People prefer what they see on TV to the rituals of their grandparents.

These are things I thought about as I went from town to town along the canal. Nobody in Gloversville makes gloves anymore. The 150 companies and 15,000 workers who made them are gone. No one makes the beautiful roll-top desks once made in Herkimer. In many of the towns along the Canal, abandoned buildings and shells of buildings are falling apart, their windows broken and door hinges rusted or gone. Several of the towns had developed slum-like sections where many run-down houses seemed to be occupied by "outsiders," people who came here just because these low cost quarters are available.

In an effort to send some "Public Works" money into Rome in the late 1950s, a Federal Grant funded the reconstruction of Fort Stanwix, a fort that in colonial times saw combat with the British, the French and the Mohawk Indians. Unfortunately the new fort was built right in the very center of town, completely upsetting the old street patterns and charm of the old city.

So now you have my expert analysis of what has happened in upper N.Y. State since I left in 1960—a kind of gloomy view for a guy who lives in a prosperous area and develops his opinions while riding a motorcycle and talking to people who tend to have "old fashioned" views...

For completeness, I must make the observation that the towns that are a bit removed from the canal route where so many immigrants had settled after the canal was built, towns where the manufacturing industry never developed, did not deteriorate as the businesses folded or moved south. With their tree lined town squares, they are almost as charming as ever. But their economic life is no longer dependant on the social and business needs of the small farms around them, and the young people tend to seek careers in other regions.

But they still enjoy their State Fairs and Firemen's Field Days.

LOCKED UP IN NIAGARA FALLS
A lady looking out a car window.

One summer, John and I carried his first son, Chris, across New York State touching some of the places I had told them about along the canal to see Niagara Falls and get a taste for what our motorcycle trips are like. (This was before we did trips with two grandsons at a time.)

As usual, when we carry one of the boys, we included a daily swim to refresh us and give us all a stretch. One of our swims was along the north edge of the Finger Lakes, in Skaneateles where the town beach is located right on route 20, my favorite road across the state. Once the main road across the state, route 20 still has many of the old motels and local bars that were the rest stops before 20 got bypassed by the N.Y. State Thruway.

While Chris scampered quickly into the lake, John and I stripped off our clothes between two cars in a parking lot and put on our bathing suits. We were tying up the strings on our suits when a lady rolled down a car window about a foot away from where we changed. She said simply, "Thanks for the show, men!" We would have offered her another look, but Chris was waiting impatiently in the lake.

The rest of the trip out to Buffalo was uneventful. We crossed into Canada and had a fancy dinner in a Canadian Hotel overlooking the falls—all lit up in rainbow colors from giant spot lights...

I almost spoiled the next day, when in the morning I broke the key trying to unlock my BMW fork lock. This caused several hours of frustration, searching for a locksmith on a Sunday. But Chris remained cheerful through the whole fiasco. It gave us time to have a leisurely breakfast after locating a locksmith through the yellow pages of the phone book. It being a Sunday morning, the locksmith took a while to fetch his truck and get to us, but he didn't seem to mind missing church.

We took the standard "Maid of the Mist" boat tour below the falls, got some pictures and headed south to visit the Ohio State Fair.

STATE FAIRS AND "FIELD DAYS"

Many of the States I have visited have annual State Fairs and County Fairs and many of the rural towns have what are called "Field Days," the latter to raise money for their volunteer fire companies.

My son, grandsons and I happen to be very fond of Funnel Cake, home made pies, Pennsylvania-Dutch food and Polish Sausage rolls—and Country Fairs are the places to get all of them. You can also get sticky with Cotton Candy, which can glue your hands to the motorcycle handlebars for weeks at a time.

I won't try to describe what you already know about State Fairs. You've seen them in the movies. I mention them here because they fit into my desire to get acquainted with country people rather than just enjoying the riding through their towns and villages.

My summer cycle trips have enabled me to enjoy visits to several County and State Fairs, including the "Festival" in Kutztown, Pa., the Delaware County Fair in Walton, N.Y. and the N.Y. State Fair in Syracuse in August. The parts that you can't fully enjoy in the TV shows include talking to the 4-H kids who take great pride in talking about their beautiful and much loved Horses, Cattle, Pigs, Sheep, Goats, Rabbits and Poultry. Unlike many young people in the city, these kids respond cheerfully visitor's questions…

And Motorcycles can park for half the car price at most Fairs.

Since I was a Volunteer Fireman myself for seven years, in Stittville, N.Y., I also enjoy attending their annual "Field Days." These are not oriented around farm animals like the County and State Fairs. They're set up in one of the town resident's pastures or empty fields, with gambling tables, food and beer tents, and sell home baked goodies—things that can raise money for their Fire Department. The people who attend are mostly from the same town and the kids are free to run loose and spend quarters to throw things, shoot at things or eat things. Fire companies from nearby towns come to join the parades that precede the opening of the grounds. Then they entertain the crowd with some competitive stuff between the various fire companies, like in tug-a-war games, rope climbing or using hoses to push each other around.

On this particular trip home from Niagara Falls, we got to the Ohio State Fair in late afternoon, ate a bunch of our favorite stuff and walked around the various exhibits before heading out to find a motel.

THE GRAVEL CHUTE

RAIN REFUGE UNDER GRAVEL CHUTE

A night or two later we were still out in central New York, on our way back from Niagara Falls and the Fair. Chris, was riding on my back seat, when a heavy rainstorm came up. Hardly able to see the road ahead (no windshield wipers) we searched desperately for cover while lightning was cracking all around. As we were entering a curve in the highway, we saw a huge iron structure—straight ahead if we ignored the turn. In desperation, John, who was in the lead, steered into it, with me right behind. It was not a good move. We found ourselves in deep gravel under a line of four or five huge funnels overhead. The funnels were loaded with gravel by tubular feed pipes and they evidently released gravel into big trucks that entered the path we came in on. The general spillage of the operation spread loose gravel all over the place. John's lighter motorcycle dug in but he kept it upright, while mine with Chris on it, started sinking into the gravel. Chris, feeling us sinking to a stop, somehow used his left pedal to launch a dive off the rear seat, while I stayed frozen to the bike and rode it to a standstill in a pile of gravel.

The huge funnels overhead provided no shelter. They were open at the top and just helped gather the rain so it could be dumped more directly on us. The pouring rain continued as we dug and pushed the bikes out of the gravel and back onto the road. We crept along the highway until we saw a huge garage on our left. We pulled in and found it was a repair facility for heavy trucks. The mechanics accepted our presence and expressed great interest in our travels, until the rain lightened enough for us to get a few miles down the road to a Holiday Inn with an indoor pool where we could sit with a bottle of premixed Manhattan cocktails and decide whether this kind of a day should be considered a "fun" one.

The next afternoon we were at Deep Creek Lake in southern Maryland. While searching for a motel, we spotted a place on the lake that rented house trailers parked along the waterfront… We got talking to a lady who was riding around the place in a golf cart. It turned out she was the manager and she let us rent a house trailer right on the waterfront. We spent an hour swimming and a "Happy Hour" chatting with her about the business of renting trailers, before walking to a nearby restaurant for dinner.

The lake is close to route 50, which provided us with a straight shot home, with a couple of short stops for coffee and souvenirs.

TRUCKERS AND RR ENGINEERS

Now we've talked about a great variety of people and how they live—but we haven't covered people who own large cross-country trucking companies or drive locomotives. On another trip I did both.

I started out west to Cumberland, West Virginia, and turned north up route 220, to revisit the Finger Lakes. It was that trip that included several of the swimming places and the "Lady Stripper" in a bar near Roaring Springs, Pa. that I mentioned in Chapter Three,

Route 220 runs north from Cumberland for a long way on one side of a beautiful valley. My first stop on that trip was in Roaring Springs, The town was formed around a powerful spring that delivers 8 million gallons of water a day, part of which is captured by a giant fountain in their Spring Lake Park in the center of town.

After a short nap on the low stone wall which surrounds the Spring Pond, I rode to the edge of town to visit the "Smith Trucking Co." They are one of the largest long-haul trucking companies in the eastern U.S. I had heard that the owner of the company had a Honda GoldWing like mine, so I drove right up to his office. We swapped stories for awhile and he took me for a tour of his huge collection of garages and dispatching facilities. It turned out that he was interested in more than motorcycles. He owned another company called "Smith Motorsports."

Smith Motorsports builds and races trucks for drag racing! They are called "semi-trucks"—and are driven by 3,000 horsepower engines! We had a great visit with the team that builds and races these machines.

Our tour of the garages ended with seeing a couple of custom made racing cars that he and his mechanics had assembled.

After an Italian dinner with him and his wife, I even got an invite to spend the night at his house.

I left in the morning and headed north for about 20 miles to Altoona, Pa. For coffee with some engineers.

THE HORSESHOE CURVE
Old locomotive drivers

Aerial View of World Famous Horseshoe Curve

In the suburbs of Altoona there is a place called "The Horseshoe Curve" where a visitor can sit in a park surrounded my steep mountains and watch a giant freight train slowly climb those mountains on a giant circle of track around him. My motorcycle and I have been there several times over the years to sit with the old time railroad engineers who gather at picnic tables there to drink their thermos of coffee and wave to the engineers driving the current trains.

ALTOONA HORSESHOE CURVE BEFORE IT BECAME A PARK

The circle of track was built in 1854 to get over the mountains without having to drag heavy loads up a steep slope—too steep to get the traction needed for the heavy loads. Even with the present slope, I have often seen multiple engines on the long trains. When I first visited in the 1950s there were only a couple of picnic tables there. In the 60s, the place was given "National Historic Park" status and a Visitors Center showed up in the 70s. In 1885 a Giant Locomotive was taken out of retirement and "restored" by volunteers for display there and in the 90s a "Railroaders Memorial Museum" appeared. The old timers around the picnic tables where I sit, quiet down as a train enters the great curve and a mood of respect, pride and affection replaces their general friendly gossip, even though a short distance away groups of Japanese are taking flash pictures of the trains that are a mile beyond the range of the flashes and lines of tourists are unloading from buses to use the bathrooms and get more bottled water.

I love that place.

TROUT RUN
Some early morning swimmers

Being in Altoona reminds me of another fun experience I had not far from here. I once stopped in a Williamsport, Pennsylvania Wal-Mart to buy a bicycle pump. I had forgotten to bring one for my air mattress. It was a hot day and I asked the man at the counter in the camping section of the store if there was a campsite with swimming nearby. He told me how to get to a place on a stream called Trout Run. I found it, set up my tent and enjoyed a very cold bath in the shallow stream called Trout Run. A local fisherman told me how to get to a nearby country bar for a few beers and dinner.

It was a Saturday night and the bar was packed three deep. What happened there was kind of special for me. As the small group I had joined began to leave at around One a.m., two couples I had told about my campsite said they would like to join me at my tent in the morning for the cold swim I had described. In turn they would bring me back to this same bar for Sunday breakfast.

The next morning the two couples came at around 8 a.m. with bathing suits under their clothes and together we coaxed another campsite couple from their morning coffee to join us in the ice cold stream water. After more-than-adequate stimulation, we finished off my fellow camper's coffee, took turns changing clothes in my tent, and all rode over to meet the other three from our Saturday night group at the same bar. After a Bloody Mary breakfast we all swore everlasting kinship and they dropped me back at my damp tent for a nap before parting.

Today I rode into that Trout Run campsite, but no one was there. No one was fishing or lounging in the stream. The campsite owner/manager remembered me and where I had pitched my tent, and the group that took that chilly swim before breakfast several years before. It occurred to me that around seven other people must remember it too.

Riding northeast from Altoona I stopped for a day in Corning, New York, just north of the Pennsylvania border. I spent most of a day touring the Corning Glass Company. I mention it here so you will know I didn't spend all my time on the road swimming and drinking beer. Corning has been in business for over 150 years and has been the leading innovator of glass products all through those years. I had no special "adventures" there, but much of my working life involved their developments in fiber optics (they still produce nearly half the fiberglass produced today). Almost all engineers of my generation once believed fiber would replace wire, cable, and microwave radio-until, that is before the advent of satellite systems.

Feeling good about knowing all this, I happily rode on to what was then the Taylor Wine Vineyards. Here the Taylor family established one of the oldest wine vineyards in the U.S. back in 1878. At the time it was the most successful winery in the world! It now has accumulated a fascinating history of ownership issues and name changes (e.g. Cellars & Bully Hill) behind it stemming from investor interests. (mostly Coca Cola) but the wine tasting—sampling—center at Keuka Lake is still there and a great place to share any kind of information that can fill a few idle hours with other wine samplers. For example, a couple of my fellow wine samplers who came from homes around the lake, especially those from Hammondsport, took turns telling me the history of a famous Hammondsport aircraft builder named Glen Hammond Curtiss. Curtiss crashed many times in Keuka Lake while developing the first practical "flying boats" (seaplanes). Curtiss became famous as "The Fastest Man on Earth" in 1907. With US Pilot License #1 the "Founder of the American Aviation Industry" built planes for what was then the War Department. The next day I confirmed what they told me about him by visiting the Curtiss Museum, but on this day at Taylor's, having just left the Corning Glass factory, I took my turn storytelling at the bar with explanations of how important glass is to our country (while they pressed me to get back to more travel stories.)

Too many friends at a wine tasting

It had been a hot and thirsty day since leaving Altoona and at the Taylor's wine tasting bar it took us all quite awhile to cover everyone's stories. By late afternoon I got confused by the variety of stories, the hot weather and by the amount of time it took to sample what seemed like dozens of varieties in Taylor's product line. I waddled out of the place ok, but had a little trouble getting on the motorcycle. I thought fuzzily about the many difficulties involved in unpacking my stuff and setting up the tent. I decided it would be best to avoid it. Too dangerous. It was already tough to remember how to get on the damned bike. And sometimes the tent ropes and bungee cords get all tangled and it's hard to tell which side of the tent is the top or the outside and where its door is. And if the tent stakes are not hammered in correctly, the tent can blow away in the night. And it hurts if the hammer hits your hand when you try to hold the stakes steady as you hammer on them. If you move your hand out of the way too quickly, the tent stake falls down before you can hit it. And besides, I forgot to go to the bathroom before I left Taylor's.

I considered going a little west to tour the Cornell Campus so I could say "I went to Cornell" sometime, but while I was in the winery my bike seemed to have developed a kind of "looseness" and a sort of mind of its own—that I thought might be dangerous. Besides, I had been to Cornell several times on previous motorcycle trips. So I got a motel about 20 miles up the road in Penn Yan. I didn't even offload my luggage at the motel; just undressed and went to sleep trying to think of new designs for glass seaplanes to carry instant wine—maybe a powdered wine. Just add water. I was smiling when I fell asleep.

In the morning I got myself invited to breakfast with a couple I used to work with who had a cottage a few miles south of Penn Yan on the East shore of the lake. My friends, Harry and Joan, were quite used to having me stop by on my summer trips, but this time I had not phoned ahead. I blamed that on my extended time at the winery. Harry and I swam awhile around their dock while Joan made some coffee for us to enjoy while we took a ride around the lake in their ski-boat and swapped memories of past visits and the time we used to work together.

From Penn Yan I went north to Lake Ontario and took the "scenic route" east along its shore—through Oswego. By mid afternoon I was ready for a nap. I slept

an hour in Selkirk State Park and swam in the lake before continuing the beautiful ride along its shore until sunset, when I got a campsite in Sackets Harbor, on
the Lake and about 8 miles from a good meal in Watertown, N.Y.

NORTHERN NEW YORK

The Sackets Harbor campsite is so beautiful and the history of the area so interesting, that I decided to wander around the village and try to meet some people—and maybe keep my campsite a second night before riding on up to
Alexandria Bay, home of the "Thousand Island Bridge."

Sackets Harbor became well known after the American Revolution. Ships
were constructed here to defend our northern boundary. If you've ever considered what real estate we acquired in the Revolution, you will have noticed that
Lake Erie, Lake Ontario and the St. Lawrence River pretty much defined our
northern boundary. In the war of 1812, the "Second War of Independence," the
British Canadians tried to break through it. Possibly because our government for-
bad trade with them (Embargo Act of 1807)—thus ending a very profitable trade
route—some of which was in booze traffic. I'll mention more on this when I ride
upstream on to Ogdensburg, N.Y.

Most people today probably remember Sackets Harbor, as a very popular
resort place in the early 1900s when rail service brought wealthy New Yorkers up
there from the city. Since WWII the popularity of places like this and other once
famous resorts in the Adirondacks has gone into a decline as wealthy vacationers
now go for air travel to extend their choices.

I rode around to the Chamber of Commerce Office, a couple of Memorials
for the War of 1812 and the Sackets Harbor Brewing Company. The latter is a
micro-brewery (make their own beer), but the atmosphere in the place was a bit
too sophisticated for my taste. And my motorcycle without the camping stuff
packed on it didn't generate any special interest…

The next morning brought more clear and sunny weather and, after a morning swim in Lake Ontario, I packed up and rode to Alexandria Bay for breakfast.
Years ago when I lived just south of here near Rome New York, I spent occasional
weekends boating, fishing and water skiing, with friends on the St. Lawrence
river, so I wasn't anxious to stay long near the bridge. Since it was still early in the
day, I rode on up the New York shore of the river to Ogdensburg, N.Y. There I
got a motel on the river and took my second great swim of the day in the almost
crystal clear St. Lawrence river. Then, before dinner, I visited the Remington
museum in Ogdensburg—you remember Frederick Remington; the sculptor

who around 1900 brought all the western cowboy and Indian characters to life in bronze. His art work made him famous and the statues he sculpted late in his career, made him rich.

The Ogdensburg museum is like a large two storey residence. It had about a half dozen rooms of Remington's art work but only one room of his statues. It also had about a dozen copies of his most popular ones—the two foot high versions. Visitors to the museum can order copies of his statues in all sizes, from about 6 inches to full size horses and riders. But the residence-like setting made it seem like it might have been a private collection that had been donated to Ogdensburg as a museum. Anyway, I got to chat with the lonesome floor workers about Remington. I learned that he was a popular writer of Westerns before he took up the art work that made him rich. Back at the motel I had dinner at the bar. I didn't get into motorcycle stories because the conversation was all about "Rum Runners" and the booming business that was built up all along the U.S. and Canadian border

During Prohibition in the early 1920s. The Prohibition Act created an illicit market for alcohol from Canada and the Caribbean. The fishing vessels in the St Lawrence River rose to the occasion and Ogdensburg was a major entry point into the U.S. The laws allowed Canadian distilleries to ship booze to a couple of Islands off the Newfoundland Coast. Small ships then brought it to the edges of U.S. territorial waters—a few miles off the U.S. shores. Small boats then ran the stuff in to the coastal towns when they saw gaps in the Coast Guard patrol runs—every night.

I heard the story about how the town's one policeman used to be called to a variety of "civil disturbances" just outside town every night, and just at the hour that the "Rum Runners" arrived. They told me the policeman was surprisingly wealthy, even though he never found reason to arrest anybody. All along the St. Lawrence I got impressions that the liquor traffic from Canada was unbelievably heavy. I had seen pamphlets at a Stowe Visitors Center in Rhode Island describing massive shipments of whiskey by mules through a winding rocky dirt trail (now a road) called "Smugglers Gap"—just north of Stowe, Vermont.

THE REAL EAST COAST

At this point I've taken you to most of the places and many of the people in central and northern New York that my motorcycle and I have visited over the years—most of them several times and on different machines. But I mustn't skip the eastern seaboard.

In the early days when I didn't make a special effort to avoid riding through or close to big cities, I tended to choose routes that would allow me to visit friends and family. This meant traveling along the east coast. I started many early trips by going right through downtown Washington (to get to the other side) and through downtown Baltimore (shorter than taking the tunnel) to use the New Jersey Turnpike and the Staten Island Ferry to pass the Statue of Liberty.

Skirting Brooklyn I wanted to ride around Floyd Bennett Field where I had once had a great experience. The field I remembered was now a giant cement slab called the John F. Kennedy (JFK) airport. Nobody at JFK today cares about the past... Too busy. So my theory about meeting people held true—the more people around you, the less people you will get to know. So here, I dealt with memories.

It was 1950 and the Korean War had just started. I had been part of a team of Hazeltine Electronics Engineers who were designing a radar that could measure the altitude of flying aircraft. The U.S. needed a "height finder" radar in Japan to help in the guidance of fighter planes that might be needed if the Chinese decided to enter war. Hazeltine was asked to ship the just built prototype height finder, along with an engineer, to Japan—as soon as possible. On two days notice, the Navy sent a cargo aircraft to Floyd Bennett Field where I had been training 6 Marine Technicians on how to assemble, operate and maintain the radar. The plane took me on a 3 month adventure to Japan, but today I just wanted to ride around the JFK airport to try and find evidence of what was there in 1950.

I found none. Only uniformed police urging me to "move along!" There was no brass plaque recording where I had loaded the first height finder ever shipped to Japan—and I couldn't pause to suck my thumb without paying "$2.00 for the first half hour."

I sped out past the "Airport Exit" sign to join the steady stream of speeding cars on the Southern State Parkway—and wondering why I had expected fond memories that only 6 other men (Marines) cared about.

THE ALLIGATOR

A map of Long Island shows it shaped a bit like an alligator with its tail on the left in Manhattan and its jaws opening about 80 miles out east in Riverhead. From there the "lower" jaw stretches on out through the Hamptons to Montauk Point. The "upper" jaw goes out to a place called Orient. Shortly after WWII I bought a house near the alligator's eyeball, in a place called Levittown, where a veteran could buy a house for $8,000 with no down payment.

I found my way to number 10 Sleepy Lane and parked my motorcycle at the curb in front of the house. As usual, a couple of children came running over from a neighbors yard to ask questions about the motorcycle…One of their moms came out to protect them from me, but we wound up spending a pleasant half hour discussing all that has changed in this famous development—like the prices going up from $8,000 to near $200,000. While we talked I was more concerned about the kids upsetting my heavily loaded motorcycle than I was with how much the 3 foot trees that Levitt originally planted have grown. (about thirty feet) But I was very impressed at how his somewhat Spartan "Town" had matured into an attractive village.

Unfortunately there was no one home at my old home, so I couldn't get in to see the upstairs rooms I had built over 50 years before. But I did see the two strips of concrete I had poured to form a driveway up to what was the original carport and is now a garage.

It had been a hot ride up from Virginia, around the JFK Airport and out to Levittown. I tried, unsuccessfully, to sweet talk my way into one of the Levittown swimming pools, as a former resident, WWII veteran, Habitat worker, ex Scout-master and Sunday school teacher, Mason, College Grad and carded AARP member. The gatekeepers would have none of it. They just yawned. This time I think the loaded motorcycle worked against me. It was in N.Y. where everybody has a scam and they figured me for just another bum. So I rode south a few miles for a short swim in the ocean at Jones Beach before getting a motel on the way to Riverhead. Next day I took the lower jaw of the alligator from Riverhead toward Montauk point.

MONTAUK POINT

In the mid 1950s, as a Hazeltine Field Engineer, I had installed a height finder radar (one like we talked about at Floyd Bennett Field) at Montauk Point—and later, while working for the MITRE Corporation, I visited the MITRE radar and Semi Automatic Ground Environment facility (SAGE, a Computer managed air defense system) at Montauk. The original village there was constructed to look like a fishing village and it still had brick buildings painted to look like homes, with windows, shutters and doors painted on—to hide the fact that it was a highly classified military facility. I was hoping to visit some of the underground complex, but the "State Park" police still prevented access to tourists. There were however the main SAGE buildings and remnants of one of the radars MITRE experimented with there. Also parts of an "antenna farm" that was once used for military communications.

Pieces of history were visible around and in the State Park, with its boarded up buildings, and old signs. It had been the home of a research effort called Hero, another called Phoenix. It had been an Army Base, a Navy Base and a State Park. British had landed there in the American Revolution as part of their landings in of New York. A half dozen gun emplacements are still there.

The only problem I faced was that after I paid the $6.00 to get into the park, I found that it had to be vacated before dark!

There are lots of motels around Montauk, but sites at the big ocean front campground in nearby Hither Hills State Park, were sold out. Without confessing to the details, I'll just say that I got a place to set up my tent amongst the sand dunes that shielded the campgrounds from high tide. I had dinner in the town.

Nobody seemed interested in my motorcycle, my luggage, my knowledge of the area's history or how I got a campsite. So I left in the morning for the Orient.

THE UPPER JAW
Talk with a famous sculptor

No—I don't mean China or even the far east. I'm talking about the Orient that is way out on the north fork of eastern Long Island, what I have labeled the upper jaw of the alligator. Instead of going back to East Hampton to take the north fork, I turned north to cross Shelter Island—which sits right in the middle of my hypothetical Alligator's jaws. It took two ferries to get me on and off Shelter Island, after which I rode on out to the isolated town of Orient.

In Orient, my wife and I have good friends named Todd (wife) and Robert Berks. Robert Berks is a very famous sculptor. He did the head of Kennedy for the Kennedy Center main lobby. He's done, Casals, Truman, Getty, Sinatra, Pope Paul, Hemmingway, Fermi, Bob Hope, Einstein, Johnny Carson, Martin Luther, Mary Beth Hume and several dozen other very notable people.

In the '70's and 80's we had become good friends while working together on conceptual designs of communities that might be completely powered by solar energy. (Even then I was meeting interesting people!) I stayed overnight with them and in the morning spent a few hours seeing his beautiful property and his huge studio. He showed me the process of designing his statues in a special clay, making molds from them and pouring liquid bronze into the molds in such a was as to push the air out of small straw-like tubes that he had carefully situated in the molds. Much of his sculpture work is giant size and he has to work while standing on giant ladders or scaffolding.

The next morning I caught the early ferry out of Orient Point for the trip across Long Island Sound to New London, Connecticut, along with travelers headed to Cape Cod and New England. I had previously visited friends on the Cape and, by ferry, Martha's Vineyard, by car with my wife. So I bypassed it and stopped just short of Boston at Plymouth Rock. I saw the Mayflower, the rock stamped 1620 and models of the first buildings in the Plymouth Colony. I re-learned what the *Mayflower Compact* was and that the Pilgrims moved here from Cape Cod. And of course there was "Speak for your self, John" Alden bringing a message from Miles Standish to Pricilla what's her name.

It has always bothered me how so many Pilgrims could base their lives and social policies on the bible when most of them couldn't read. Some of them figured it was OK for a man to have several wives and almost all of them figured how to make sure the more ambitious guys had to share whatever they managed to produce.

It was a fascinating stop, but I failed to establish any personal contact. Too many tourists! I went on through Boston and Cambridge to the Colonial Inn in Concord. There I had the first "Flintlock Special" I'd had since I retired from the nearby MITRE Corporation in 1989. (Bourbon, doctored with White Crème de Menthe and Grenadine)

In the morning I walked to the nearby Concord Bridge where the first shot of the American Revolution was reportedly fired. Leaning on the railing over the Concord River, I sat with George Washington as he wondered whether Hays would be able to drag the cannons from Ticonderoga over the snow and ice to get them to Dorchester Heights to push the British out of Boston[4]. When it occurred to me that it had actually happened—and turned out to give us rebels the courage to go on with the war, I was stirred up enough to leave this peaceful place and take the beautiful ride from Concord to Bedford.

I spent the rest of the day visiting my friends at MITRE in Bedford Mass. I had worked for MITRE fir 29 years.

We'll come back to MITRE in Chapter XII after my windshield breaks and slams into my chest.

---

4.   McCullough, David. *"1775"*.Simon & Schuster 2005

5

WEST VIRGINIA AND KENTUCKY

Remember all that stuff in my Introduction about morphing into one's more complete self after the mind drops all the regular patterns it uses to cope with one's daily routines? When you're motorcycling alone, away from your job, your "to do" lists, and your social calendar, you can give your imagination some time to just troll for things to think about. In my case I find myself dealing with some form of introspection, usually relating to existing concerns that need more thought. This process tends to create a moody state of mind, but then my imagination kicks in to help transition my thinking away from my well exercised concerns. Imagination can take you anywhere,—to carnal, spiritual, or even supernatural ideas.

You will note that there are touches of these processes in many parts of my recollections. For example, consider my visit to—

A COAL TOWN IN WEST VIRGINIA
Families of Coal Miners

In 1996 I made a trip through Kentucky. On the initial leg of the trip, near Beckley, West Virginia, I saw a sign for Kopperston. It triggered my memory of an interesting article from a National Geographic magazine about an isolated in-the-mountains coal town a little west of Beckley. It was one of many company-built "Coal Towns." This one was built from scratch as a "model coal camp" by Kopper Coke, one of the Mellon Companies where, as Tennessee Ernie Ford said, residents owed their souls to the company store. Miners didn't own their homes and could be evicted—and many were evicted by the coal companies during the coal strikes of early nineteen twenties—just as I was entering the world. Ah yes, I remember it well.

It seems like all the roads in this part of the world are two-lane roads, chained together with blind curves and no passing signs., The roads seem to be loaded with big coal trucks, all in first gear whether going up a 9% grade or downhill. In fact, based on my own observations, I'd guess that 95% of all road traffic west of Beckley, West Virginia, is made up of coal trucks. (The other 5% are pickups with rifles mounted in the rear view window and a hound dog riding in the back. They ride in the left lane no matter what is coming and invent swerving moves as needed to avoid collisions.)

It was a hot day as route 85 spiraled down toward "town" between the close packed mountains that looked like giant upside-down ice cream cones." Winding through them, I thought of the bird that flew down in ever decreasing circles until it flew up its own rear end—but that's too crude to mention here.

Slowing down as I passed an old sign that said "Entering Kopperston," I shifted into neutral and coasted for several blocks, to get down to the speed limit. With the motorcycle in neutral I soaked up the strangely quiet charm of the many simple little houses built in 1938, and packed together in a straight line on a piece of flat land between the sharply rising mountains on the left and right of the road.

A FIELD OF DREAMS

I saw no gas station but found a coke machine in front of a small store that was closed. Unable to ride with one hand, I was sitting with the coke on a curb along the old slate sidewalk and studying the houses across the street, when I spotted between them some broken wood bleachers and the wired backstop of an old baseball field. I walked over between the houses and on to the old ball diamond, now completely overgrown with tall grass. My mind jumped to the Kevin Costner movie, "Field of Dreams" as I trudged through the tall grass to sit a few minutes on the broken down bleachers along the first base line.

In the dead quiet my mind began putting men on the old field. Looking at that old wood-framed backstop now held up primarily by the anchor fence-type webbing behind home plate, I started hearing the "thunks" of baseballs in those old fat catcher's mitts,—and even some vague cheers and boos of bygone parents, wives, sisters, girlfriends—the families of coal mine workers now long gone. Heavy field grass hadn't yet grown around the hard ground at home plate where every player got to stand and wiggle his feet and his rear end as he settled into his batting pose. There were still somewhat less-bald spots showing the base positions and where the infield had played. A surviving worn path to first base suggests that the pitching wasn't all that good.

As I speculated on this, I was suddenly brought back to life by the "caw-caw" of some crows who flew in to view discussing this stranger sitting on their bleachers. I, of course, apologized to them for trespassing and promised not to leave the coke can as I left.

I was returning from the field to my motorcycle, passing between the closely spaced small houses, when an elderly woman gave me a fright. She spoke to me as I came from behind her house to pass alongside one end of her small half-porch. She hadn't been there when I parked my bike on the curb across from her house, but here she was now on her porch with a mug of coffee or tea in her hand. She said she had seen me coast to the curb and walk behind her house.

At first it was a bit difficult for me to explain why I wanted to sit in the bleachers of an abandoned ball field. She probably thought I was looking for a potty stop—but she warmed to my curiosity about Kopperston and my sentimental observations about the ball field. Once again the motorcycle itself broke the ice. If I had been in a car she probably would have called the sheriff rather than investigating on her own.

Somehow she got me talking about my family and I got the impression that since I had a family, I must be OK to talk to. I observed that the town was surprisingly attractive for a coal town—dead, but attractive with its neat rows of small houses. This started a wonderful conversation, interrupted only once when she went inside to pour me a cup of coffee.

She shared some of her memories. The community was very proud of the town. It was built by "Koppers Coal Mines". Amongst the "Coal Camps" of the nation it was considered "Top of the Line." They considered Kopperston as having two "Camps." The "Upper Camp" (where we were) and the "Lower Camp" a mile or so south through "21 Holler"—called that because there were 21 houses in a row on the way. I think this two-camp idea stemmed from two main entrances to the mines, called "Tipples"—where the coal cars coming up from the mines dumped their loads onto trucks or trains. In the years when the men were shipping out two trains a day, each with 150 cars full of coal, the town was coated with black dust. and houses had to be swept clean every day.

Because I showed so much interest in the detailed history of the town, she referred me to a librarian in Oceana, the next town south, a Mrs. Glenna Brown. (I contacted Glenna later to try and get the name and address of my new friend. Glenna made some guesses, but more importantly, she too was raised in Kopperston. She too became my friend and together with her friend, Paul Blankenship, expanded greatly on what I had learned.)

Glenna remembered how Koppers ran a daily bus to where they had built a Company Store in Oceana, a store that delivered to the Camps whatever was purchased on these bus trips. The company houses were leased to the miners who were paid in company "Script"—round coins with a "K" in the center.

The company retained ownership of the water wells, the electric utilities and the food store. They all lived in debt. Everyone owed the company money under a "credit system" and there was seldom any money left after debts were settled on paydays. Glenna said that on many paydays, many miners couldn't draw anything. The Company Store was demolished a year or so before I got there.

Things improved during each of the World Wars, when the demand for coal skyrocketed, but union organizing activities after WWI ended caused the deaths of many miners.

She said there are no longer many couples with children in Kopperston, although later, as I left town, I did see a lot of clothes being exchanged in yard sales. She might have been comparing today to past days when many of the now empty houses were full of families. I was touched deeply by her talk about the anxieties in the lives of families who had men in the mines. Since the whole village lived as one big family, everyone suffered together when there was any kind of accident or if any member was evicted from his home.

As this rather personal information was exchanged, a kind of friendly intimacy developed, and she felt free to ask me about my unusual, and what she considered odd, curiosity about her town. She said that in her 20 plus years there, no outsider had ever even slowed down, much less stopped to talk to residents. This led to her underlying questions:—what the heck are you doing riding all around the country without your wife, and why stop in Kopperston?

I fumbled with answers, but she seemed to accept that the world does include people like me. And she recognized my interest in history and as I mentioned above, offered that for more information about Kopperston's history, I should contact Ms. Glenna Brown.

Being with this friendly, but lonesome, lady in this quiet and peaceful place planted in a history of troubles, hardships and pain, was a rich experience for me. I use the word "rich" to cover a range of emotions that are too complex to describe.

As I rose from the porch I was already wondering whether she thought of me as a sort of hobo, or just a very confused character, "riding around the country

without his wife." But a mile or so down the road, I decided it made no difference. We had become friends.

It was now after noon and quite hot. Checking my map, I could only find one
lake between me and the Kentucky border: Bailey Lake. So I headed for it on
route 97. Like Kopperston, most of the little towns I went through had only a
few streets parallel to the one I was on and very few side streets. The roads are in
the very narrow crotches where the mountains meet, where there is only room for
the one road along one side of the winding stream that carries the run-off from
the irregular intersections of the mountains. In many places only a single jagged
line of houses can fit beside the main stream.

The landscaping is fascinating if you aren't in a hurry. Depending on which
side of the road has a sufficiently level place to build a house, about half the
homes have a wooden bridge to cross the stream that the road follows. Picture
hundreds of old rickety bridges that don't look as if they could carry a modern
car. And, in places where there's no level room next to the stream, many homes
have steep dirt driveways like mini versions of the runaway truck ramps that are
everywhere throughout the mountains.

I've mentioned that many of the houses seemed to have continuous yard sales
in progress. These are not your typical Saturday morning events. It was a week
day. Since there is little traffic here, these must be primarily exchanges of clothes
and shoes amongst local people as children grow, or people die. It could be the
main mechanism for social interaction, i.e., at each sale location there were either
a few women clustered together or there was no one sitting with the merchandise.
Nobody sat alone.

Slanting overhead across the roads through these mining towns there are occasional shiny aluminum tubes, four to six feet in diameter. Inside the tubes there
are large rubber belts which carry raw coal to huge screens, or sieves, which shake
out the small stuff and drop it on another belt in another tube, which goes to the
overhead coal bins where rail cars are loaded. Other tubes carry the coarser coal
that didn't go through the screens, to grinders; more screening, more tubes, and
even more grinders. The kluge of tubes makes one think of a futuristic amusement park or maybe a bunch of water slides that have been redistributed by a tor-
nado.

I enjoyed that afternoon ride beside the stream which competes with a rail line
for space in the notches between the steep mountains from Kopperston through
Oceana, Coal Mountain, Clear Fork, Baileysville, and along route 25 to Bailey
Lake. It's a low income area with lots of old 1950s and 1960s pick-up trucks and
small family vegetable gardens planted next to clotheslines full of overalls. There

were no megastores, restaurants, bars, movies or commercial tourist attractions. No golf courses. No noise but from the birds, the gurgle of the water around the rocky places in the stream, an occasional barking dog, and the comforting hum of my motorcycle engine. In fact, while daydreaming, I forgot to look for a swimming place as I went by Bailey Lake.

I rode along feeling an emotion I can't put into words. I was moved by the bleak but peaceful way of life here; the feeling of a sort of privacy buried along this stream through the mountains. Coming from a world where every need or wish is satisfied by purchasing something, I was impressed by the Spartan but somehow complete nature of this unique culture buried in these mountains.

Was it a culture I would be comfortable in? Or would it change because someone like me joined it?

To some extent the difference from things I'm used to made the area seem a bit uncivilized and it made me think of Alfred North Whitehead's observation that, "The major advances in civilization are processes which all but wreck the societies in which they occur." Certainly the things associated with the "civilized" way of life would fracture the society that has evolved here. It struck me that the history of the Shawnee and Cherokee Indians illustrates this theory. They once hunted here. They massacred most of the settlers who tried to displace them. The Indians didn't mine coal. Neither could they make a buck from the settlers. So they could only deal with each other.

They must have been the ones who started the Yard Sales.

WILLIAMSON, KENTUCKY

Leaving West Virginia to cross the Kentucky border into Williamson, Kentucky, I instinctively started looking for the Jack Daniels distillery. That was dumb. Jack is made in Tennessee. (Did you know that any whiskey labeled "Bourbon" must come from the corn and spring waters of Bourbon County, Kentucky? If you got that right, how about this: Bourbon County is dry!)

Coasting downhill into Williamson was like getting an aerial view of a large railroad yard. The road ended in a confusion of streets and a hodgepodge of buildings. I stopped in a gas station and looked around for an idea on how to learn about the place. That was when I saw the "House of Coal." "House of Coal"

THE HOUSE OF COAL
A retired Major who loves history

It was carved out of a huge rectangular block of coal in 1933. Best I can remember it is about 15 feet high, 30 feet wide and about 40 feet deep. They hollowed out a single room and lined it with wood for a Chamber of Commerce office. Over the front door it says, "Tug Valley Chamber of Commerce." The coal house struck me as rather silly, but it is probably a better tribute to the area's past than a statue of a coal miner being clubbed by a company-hired "detective" would be. More on this in a minute.

Inside the coal house sat a one-man Chamber of Commerce, a retired army officer who hadn't seen anyone from the outside world in months—at least not anyone interested in Williamson's history. I read a pamphlet or two and learned that in the 1800's, Williamson, which had river and canal access to the Susquehanna River before there were roads leaving towns, was known as "The Lumber Capitol of the World," and "a City of Millionaires." With lumber money, the "Lumber Barons" built huge majestic homes many of which are still there. Dirt roads began to appear in the late 1770's and the Lumber Barons built one of the earliest horse-drawn streetcar systems in America in 1865. The streetcars of course were operated profitably by the Barons.

With the coming of automobiles just after World War One, the trolley business got less profitable. At the same time, the railroads began to cut into the water transportation advantage that Williamson had; its access to the Susquehanna River and out to the Atlantic ocean.

With this much background together with what I had learned from the lady in Kopperston, I got the lonesome attendant talking and found him to be something of an expert on the "mine wars" which took place in this area, the southwest corner of West Virginia around where Kopperston and Williamson are located.

During World War One there was a coal boom and wages paid to miners increased somewhat, especially in the more populated eastern part of the State. When the mine operators cut wages after the war, the miners, stimulated by the

United Mine Workers Union, made attempts to organize their concerns. The mine owners, with help from hired "detectives" from the Baldwin-Felps Company, began to evict from their homes the miners who were promoting the formation of unions. These mountain people, many of whom were veterans of the recent war, all had rifles. Chaos followed from 1917 to 1921.[1]

A popular police chief, Sid Hatfield, was involved in the killing of some Felps agents who were evicting miners from their company-owned homes. So the coal companies had their agents murder the unarmed Hatfield on the steps of a courthouse where he was reporting for trial. Naturally he became a folk hero.

Because so many miners went on strike and were evicted from their homes, the coal mine owners brought in European immigrants and southern blacks as "strike breakers" to replace them. The displaced miners formed armies and organized "tent colonies." Because of the strikers continuing disruption of mining operations, Federal troops were brought in by the influential mine operators to "restore order," and the Federal troops established "Mineguard Camps."

The various troop movements were all by railroad and came through Williamson. Here and near here, the unemployed miners greeted them as enemies. RR tracks got torn up. The Federal troops from their "mineguard camps" raided the miners in their "tent colonies" and vice-versa. Lots of people got shot, but strangely, almost no records of miner deaths were recorded.

In the so-called "Mingo County Wars," the Federal Government actually sent in Jimmy Doolittle to manage a 14 bomber attack on an estimated 5,000 man army of miners in tent colonies with bombs loaded with nails and metal fragments. The miners were supplied with arms by the United Mine Workers of America, the UMWA. The evicted miners identified themselves with red bandannas. (This was the origin of the term "Rednecks!)

Strikes and shootings led to additional Federal troops being brought in, and the UMWA-backed efforts to unionize the miners weren't effective until Roosevelt addressed the problem under the "New Deal".

All this chaos was similar to what happened to a great variety of workers trying to form unions in the Silver Mines in Idaho, the Steel Facilities in Pennsylvania, the Pullman RR and later in the Ford Plants in Michigan.

---

1.   Laurie, Clayton D. *The U.S. Army and the Return to Normalcy in Labor Disputes Intervention: The Case of the West Virginia Coal Mine Wars.* West Virginia History. Division of Culture and History, 50,*1991*

THE HATFIELDS AND MCCOYS

No other visitors had come in the House of Coal, so my "Coal House" host went on with more recent history of his home town. He repeated that Williamson had once been a prosperous transportation hub where coal was moved out of the mountains. Today it's on hard times and the Chamber of Commerce has been trying to think of ways to promote tourism. The history of the lumber business, the first street cars and the "Mine Wars" do not attract tourists. (I'm an exception) The main attraction for tourists is the list of the sites where the famous Hatfields and McCoys killed one another over a period of 50 years starting in the 1860s.

Blood vengeance was the only law in these remote areas and tourists love bloody stories. The Hatfields and McCoys were Christians, so they felt that "when one of mine gets killed, at least two of yours have got to be killed." Just killing one for one is like forgiving the debt! Besides, killing promotes tourism. So in Kentucky they dug a hell of a lot of graves for a body to visit.

Neither the Hatfields nor the McCoys restricted their killings to each other's families. As mentioned earlier, Sid Hatfield helped kill several coal company detectives who were trying to evict miners from their homes in Matawan. Thus it became OK to kill detectives working for the coal companies.

I told the Coal House guy he should write a book. In the couple of hours I was there, nobody else came in to pick up brochures or ask questions. And I found no postcards of Williamson to take home.

ENGINE TROUBLES

Leaving the House of Coal, I headed rather indirectly west toward a campground in Prestonsburg, hoping for a cool-down swim in Dewey Lake. At the lake I got my swim next to a sign in the no-one-in-sight marina area that said "No Swimming." It was too early to set up in the campground so, in a wet bathing suit, I then went southwest on superhighway 80 at a high speed with the idea of tenting in the "Daniel Boone National Forest."

I didn't make it.

As the day began to close, the highway heat rose to around a hundred degrees. I raised my speed to match. That's when the bike started complaining. It started reducing power and backfiring. By the time I got to Hazard, Kentucky, (an appropriate name for what follows) I was struggling between second and first gear to keep the machine moving while I looked for a motel. Jerking down the road and backfiring was bad enough to cause some snickering along my route, and serious damage to my image. Motorcycle riders are supposed to travel fast with a loud but steady sound, not with engine coughs, explosive backfiring and jerks. And not when they are riding dressed in bathing trunks that are not embossed with the "Harley Davidson" logo.

Now years of management experience have developed in me the habit of never dealing directly or intelligently with a problem. First you sublimate it so you can present a macho attitude and say "It's no big deal!" In this case: I first decided that the problem must be due to rust and water in my gas. I thought it must have been that last gas station. I thought that cashier looked anxious about something when she saw me changing from my damp bathing suit to dry shorts. So I bought two cans of Dry-Gas and added them to the tank. Then I jerked my sick machine to a motel, checked in and walked to a nearby Italian restaurant where the cold beer helped me suppress the proper problem solution into my sub-conscious. I was aware that I had stuffed into my subconscious three theories on what the problem was. I had already eliminated Theory I, i.e. the water-in-the-tank theory. Water doesn't cause backfires! But my highly trained conscious mind continued with the macho "No Problem" attitude as I drifted into sleep with thoughts about what the lady in Kopperston had said—something about wandering around without my wife.

Two friendly maids

After optimistically checking out of the motel at 6:30 the next morning I had a little trouble starting the motorcycle, but rationalized that the dry gas hadn't yet gotten through the fuel pump. About four miles out, the machine angrily declared that "Theory I was incorrect you dummy!" I had to quietly mutter an irreligious expression and make a U-turn to go back and deal with my subconscious, where the real cause of the trouble was stored. But it held back the real solution and released Theory II; an exhaust valve is staying open, giving me low compression in one cylinder, therefore low power and unburned gas is getting into the hot mufflers and exploding into the embarrassing backfires.

It was so early that the motel gave me back my room key. So I got a chair from my room, set it by the bike, got a cup of coffee from the motel lobby, and sat quietly for a minute thinking about what I had read in Zen and the Art of Motorcycling ten years ago. Author, Robert Pirsig's Chautauqua on "stuckness," i.e. being stuck, advises: *Losing patience leads to anger. Anger leads to mistakes. Peace of Mind isn't just nice to have when doing technical work, it's the whole thing. You can't do things correctly without it.* I think Pirsig said that one must cultivate an inner quietness so that one's goodness can shine through—but I may have gotten that idea from some old Baptist hymn. Anyway, I calmly removed the valve covers, checked and reset the valves on both sides, and tried to smile as I replaced the covers while suffering with The Bad News: All the valve gaps had been quite fine.... I had to (calmly) address Theory III.

This was the theory I hated to think about. Fortunately, by now the two busy motel maids working in the rooms near mine sensed my need for sympathy and adopted a "poor-lad-so-far-from-home" viewpoint. I continued to feign confidence as one of them brought me another cup of coffee from the lobby. I was hot and the coffee increased my sweating but I delighted in the special attention.

By now I was of course in love with both maids. They brought me 2 large white towels to replace the two from my room that now lay on the pavement under my bike. They also arranged a late check out so I could get a last minute shower. I proceeded as if my two false theories were just part of one grand procedure to fix the sick machine—and that I was some sort of genius mechanic.

They were very impressionable. (I had asked them earlier if they knew that Kentucky had given birth to two Presidents: Lincoln and Jeff. Davis. They said no and that I was very smart to know such a thing. And who, they asked, was Jefferson Davis?

That spoiled my plan to further impress them with the fact that Kentucky supplied troops to both sides in the civil war, sort of like today's lobbyists giving money to both candidates in an election. But I feared they might ask, "Who did we fight in the Civil War?"

Theory III was that the points were worn down and not opening enough. This means there is not enough time for current through the coil (or in this case two coils) to build up a sufficient electromagnetic field that will collapse and cause the spark plugs to fire in whatever cylinder the distributor is pointing to. (On my BMW they use two coils, one for each cylinder, so no distributor is needed. Both cylinders fire together, but only the one that is at the top of its compression stroke has any effect. The other is in an "exhausted" cylinder.) What causes the "backfiring" symptom is the weak spark not always firing and letting the gas mixture move on into the hot muffler where it "explodes."

Unlike Theories I and II, this Theory doesn't allow me to sit in a chair while I address it. It's not like with an old car where you can raise the hood, unsnap the distributor cap and adjust the points. On my BMW you have to remove the horn mounting bar, loosen the crash bars, disconnect the battery, and lie on your back to remove a large "belly" casting that covers the ignition points assembly. Only then can you remove the centrifugal spark advance mechanism to get to the breaker points.

Lying on my back on the nice fresh towels, I replaced and set the proper gaps on a new set of points that I always carry on the motorcycle. I got the whole damned thing back together, took a cool shower and put on my most endearing smile to properly express my very real appreciation to the two maids. Then I washed my face and hands and accelerated smartly down the driveway into the Kentucky Mountains.

Well, at this rate we'll never get to an end of the trip. Westward Ho! No time to review my musings traveling on the Daniel Boone Parkway through the Daniel Boone National Park from Hazard to Somerset. Remembering that Daniel told the colonists there were so many turkeys in Kentucky that there wasn't room for them all to fly at the same time, I made a special effort to be alert in case they launched.

SO MUCH FOR HAZARD, KENTUCKY

Did you know that in the 1800s most roads in Kentucky were built with private funds and most were toll roads? I saw some of the toll houses that still exist but I didn't check to see if they wanted a toll payment.

I turned south at Somerset and rode to Burnside, to check out the fancy house boats that are rented out by the week on huge Lake Cumberland. The lake was inviting and my bike troubles had caused me to forget to dry my damp bathing suit in the Hazard motel from the Dewey Lake swim. It was still in the outside pocket of my duffle bag. Who could blame me for changing into it behind the marina's "No Swimming" sign and taking a swim.

Houseboats fascinate me. Not the ones with kids swimming around them. I like to imagine what goes on in the ones I occasionally see anchored out in a lake with all shades closed and wafting romantic music across the water. Have they replaced the old places where we used to park in dad's car at night with places that provide privacy in the daytime? Or are they just an additional "opportunity."

I rode through a small part of the Cumberland National Park and after a coffee and a short walk around the charming arts-and-crafts town called Berea, I headed north for Lexington, the city of "Horse Mania."

DANIEL BOONE

BOONE, W.VA,

On the way up to Lexington I came on one of those "Hysterical Site" signs (I don't see or spell too good) pointing to the site of Fort Boonesborough which was originally built by Daniel 'his-self'—with help from a couple of fellow explorers. I had visited Boone, West Virginia where there is no trace of Daniel except on a totem pole, but I found him in Boonsborough, Kentucky.

Daniel preferred the wilderness to life in Washington—as long as he was able to get a white woman to travel this far west. (He was the first to succeed) He fought with Indians frequently. He lived with indians for months. He rescued his kidnapped daughter from Indians and was adopted as a son of an Indian Chief.

He built a fort made up of a square of 26 cabins with their backs facing the Indian threat and their fronts facing a central square. His life is a fascinating story.

Having dawdled too long in Boonesboro, I skipped a planned stop at Mary Todd Lincoln's house in Lexington in favor of searching, unsuccessfully, for a hotel with a big porch where I could enjoy a Kentucky mint julep before dinner. So I cruised around the city checking out the statues of horses that are all over Lexington, some colored green, some red and some in five colors—and headed east on Interstate 64 to camp in Morehead, Kentucky.

Now loaded with stories of coal towns, mine wars and Daniel Boone adventures—oh yes, and a story of two kind maids at a motel, I decided to take the fast roads toward home the next day. I crossed the Ohio River at Huntington and made it to Elkins, West Virginia. Here's a place I can use to finish my classification of bar types started in Chapter III.

THE THIRD KIND OF BAR

As you have seen, I'm not always successful in locating a place to camp and swim that is near the kind of rural community bar I described in Chapter Three. But since I am usually quite a ways from a city, I often wind up in a resort area of some sort. In these places I find my third kind of bar—much different from either the "country bar" or "the city bar" I described earlier. I call these "resort bars." Elkins has a typical one.

Traveling east from Lexington, Kentucky, first on Interstate 64 to Cumberland and northeast up 79 on another very hot day, I decided that I needed an afternoon swim. I decided on Stonewall Jackson Lake, where there is a campground. But before I got to the lake, I saw a sign for a motel with an indoor pool. An air conditioned night sounded good, so I turned east on 33 to Elkins, West Virginia.

On the edge of the popular Monongahela National Forest, Elkins attracts hikers, bikers, canoers, and a variety of others seeking fun in the out-of-doors. I know it attracts hundreds, because I met half of them playing happily in the motel pool.

I spent the evening drinking with the rest of them in a crowded Elkins Bar. Together we spent enough to enable the pay-off of a large part of the mortgages on four Elkins bars.

In Chapters Three and Six we mentioned bars like these; bars located in vacation spots or where outdoorsmen gather. Unlike in the rural bars—in these resort bars the patrons seldom know each other, although they all travel with companions. The clientele are all in a friendly mood. A good percentage of them come from cities where even their neighbors are strangers, so these types enjoy making new friends when they are on vacation. (In general, the girls are more attractive in these bars than those in the country and city bars. (Maybe very attractive girls get more invites to resorts than the ordinary girls do.)

It is in these resort bars that a talented bar tender can make the place the most popular one in town. These bars do not generally have daily "regulars"—other than the sweetheart of the bar tender-and the guys who come in to check out the visiting folks. The local population avoids these bars because they tend to be expensive "tourist places." But they do have a more-or-less guaranteed clientele if they are "the only game in town," and usually a tourist population that's far from home and wanting to "get out" for the evening.

The customers come in wanting to socialize and spend the evening, but, unless drunk already, they are a bit shy about initiating a conversation—until a "party" atmosphere can be established. The good bartender, often the owner, knows how to build such an "atmosphere."

First he or she tries to find out where a couple of his or her customers are from, even if it's only to the nearest State. Usually a, "where yuh' from?" routine is adequate. Then all that is needed is to make this information known to someone else at the bar who has lived in, or near, or even has friends, in one of these places. (Veterans of WWII remember the U.S.O. girls who always started the first dance with "Where You from?" and then "I danced with a guy who said he was from New York State last week. His name was Frank. Any chance you knew him?")

The bartender does not transfer information privately, one-on-one. He just wants to introduce a possible topic for discussion. He does it just loud enough for all to hear while he casually washes a glass or mixes a drink, "Hey Chicago. You got a buddy down here," or "Hey Boston, here's another Red Sox fan" as he nods from one to the other. Others at the bar hear this exchange and often as not, chime in criticizing the team's current standing, or offering, "I passed through there when I was in the navy."

At this time there is no anxiety about interrupting a private conversation. Anyone can jump in.

As I've said, you find this kind of bar at vacation spots, on Cruise Ships or on the beaches of the Caribbean. I've found them in the Adirondacks, in the lake regions of Wisconsin and Michigan, and in other vacation places like Elkins.

One comment on the "where you from?" approach to starting a conversation—the most common and effective ice breaker in many social situations. It's fine in the small town bars, but it's not my favorite in the resort bars. You can understand that I prefer the ones where the bartender opens with, "Here's another motorcycle guy!" It might surprise you, but I've found that almost everyone, even the most insouciant guy at the end of the bar, has a motorcycle story. It starts with the identification of someone who "used to have a Harley" or "used to love to ride on the back of a Harley".

Whatever the topic, the bartender is successful if it leads to a group having dinner together at some table in the bar—because nobody wants to leave the "party". On this occasion, the Elkins bar was full of bicycle riders, hikers and kayakers and conversations formed around these interests. I had little to offer, but enjoyed hearing stories at a table of people I had met in the pool when I first arrived. I went to bed quite late that night.

In the morning I arose early, with no desire for food. After several days of very hot weather I found it was chilly climbing route 33 up into the mountains of the Monongahela National Forest. Coming east, I rode into a fiercely bright early morning sun flashing through the roadside trees and mixing fiercely bright and black shadow patterns on the road, like the crazy blotches used in Rorschach tests. The winding road made these fierce flashes from the sun switch these road patterns from left to right and back ahead of me. It felt like batteries of strobe lights from all directions were pointed directly at my scratchy sun glasses, making me wonder where the road was, and if I was about to run off it into the woods or crash into a big pot hole.

The impact of the flashing may have been influenced by last night's fellowship in the Elkins bar together with two days of highway riding in the hot sun, any of which may have fried what little was left of my brain. I guided my course by the occasional notch in the sky line between the trees on either side of the road ahead, whenever the road was straight enough to provide a notch. Navigating by the skyline made me exceedingly anxious about hitting a pot hole which would be indistinguishable in the road patterns. I dropped my speed to about 5 mph.

Still, the flashing made me dizzy, and I began to think about what the man up in Canada with the cross had told me about God trying to contact me. Could this be Him?

Slowly the sun rose higher and fewer trees participated in the torture. I finally began to get glimpses of the road. Could it be that my acknowledgement of that conversation in Canada was enough of a contact?

The winding road now slowly favored the south as I wound down the mountain, shaking a bit from the tension the strobe lights had caused. But the temperature had now risen and the sweater and jacket I had put on earlier, together with the anxiety, made me think about a swim to clear my head and restore my appetite. Still on route 33, I finally bumped into the South Branch of the Potomac River at Seneca Rocks.

SENECA ROCK
More kids swimming

I had tent camped at Seneca Rocks before. Some kids with towels had guided me to what's got to be one of Virginia's best swimming holes, where the South Branch of the Potomac makes a wide and five foot deep curve below the famous cliffs whose jagged tops outline the profile of an Indian's face. The vertical cliffs on one side of the pool define the inside of the curve that forces the river to wash out the far side to form a beautiful clear pool as it turns. The pool is floored with clean creek-stones, all smooth from tumbling along the river bed and getting washed by the clear mountain water which hasn't had a chance to flow through farm or pasture lands with mud banks. Each stone would easily qualify as a collectors item if they weren't free. Just walking barefoot on those smooth stones pleases me.

Generations of kids, like me, have swung from a great rope swing that hangs from a giant tree at Seneca. The opposite bank of the river is dense with grass, trees and vines, except for a beach of creek stones kept clean by the river when at high water, it makes the turn around the cliffs, overshoots this bank and sweeps out the poorly rooted young greenery, to give us kids a place to leave our shoes and clothes. You can understand why I never pass through Seneca Rock without a swim and a rope swing with my young friends, and today was no exception. There are not many things as refreshing as a cool swim before breakfast.

seneca rock swimming hole

As you would expect, the path from the pool out of the woods is well worn by generations of kids. The dirt is hard around the protruding rocks in the path. On the heavy motorcycle I eased slowly along it in first gear, legs extended to handle the unbalancing of the bike as its tires slid sideways off the rocks into the ruts in the path. When I got to a place that I could horse the thing around, I faced the motorcycle back out and left it there while I took a refreshing swim. I put on some "going home" clothes and thought about breakfast.

A new breakfast place, a few hundred yards south along the river, has replaced the old one I had visited in the past. It's just across the street from the old, abandoned place which was on the river side of the road, so the old place blocks the view of the river from the new place. When everything around you is beautiful, nobody seems to care about preserving a view.

Anyway, good feelings revived in me as I entered the new place fresh from the cool swim and saw fried eggs, fried bacon, fried potatoes, fried pancakes, and coffee, on the only occupied table in the place.

I thought it would be unfriendly for me to sit alone at a table, when there was only one other customer in the place, a truck driver. So I plunked down with my full plate next to his. His was the big diesel truck, idling noisily outside—the one despoiling the sacred quiet of Seneca valley.

I had ordered the same big "special" breakfast that my latest friend was having and he accepted me like I was kinfolk. He told me about the motorcycle he used to have, and launched into a lecture on the incompetent truck drivers burning their brakes coming down the steep and winding road I had just descended on. I nodded a lot to show I was listening, while I wiped the big warm plate clear with the last of my toast,—somehow feeling in a hurry because of the noise his truck was making in the quiet valley. As I mounted my bike, I noticed the smell of burned brakes around his truck.

The trip home from Seneca Rocks was very familiar to me, but after having been a couple of weeks away from home, the trip was a lot more exciting than just returning from a day trip for a swim.

6

TRAVELING COMPANIONS

After each of my annual trips my friends back home have enjoyed asking questions about, my "adventures." And almost every year I get a couple of requests from friends who would like to accompany me on a trip. In the '1970s it was always a pleasure to have my son, John, for company. And in the '80's I enjoyed occasionally taking his sons, my grandsons, on trips. We'll talk about the trips with grandsons later.

Other than those trips with my son, I have preferred to travel alone. The routines that I have mentioned have made it uncomfortable for me to adapt to the interests of other riders who generally aren't interested in nightly bar conversations, tenting, swimming or traveling without a schedule. And besides, I need to tell some stories to make new friends, and other people might get tired of hearing them. And dealing with rain is very upsetting for occasional riders. Only my son seems to like my ideas of what makes a fun trip.

Traveling with my son is so different from traveling with others that to avoid some of the generalizations I always make, I'll talk about it separately. Then I'll tell you about a few of the exceptions I made to my "travel alone" policy and how they worked out.

MY FRIEND SAM

During this, my 2003 trip, and supposedly my "last," my mind keeps going back to past trips with my son, John, and an old motorcycling companion named Sam, whom I've already mentioned in Chapter Three. The three of us often went on trips together in the early years.

Sam was a friend since we were in the sixth grade together.(1936) We separated during WWII, but kept in touch by mail. When he got a motorcycle we arranged to make some trips together and each summer after I moved to Virginia in the 1960s, we would arrange for him to cycle northwest from his home in

Paterson, New Jersey, to meet me, and sometimes John, at my parent's small farm between Delhi and Andes in upstate New York, to join for an annual ride.

To put it bluntly, Sam was a pain in the ass to travel with. He liked the comforts and good times we always had at my parent's farm and he usually had a couple of problems with his motorcycle that needed attention; problems like "It don't run right." Or, "It's hard to start." So we would roll his bike into the barn and address these problems—interspersed with sleeping in feather beds, dinners with fresh corn from mom's garden, dad's morning flap jacks and sausage or fresh trout, and swims in the river that runs through my dad's farm. Sam was a commercial truck driver and this taste of the good life would always dampen his enthusiasm for going on to the frequent "inconveniences" of travel by motorcycle.

Once we got Sam on the road, he wouldn't sleep in a tent, hated to pay a share of the motel bill, and had to stop every half hour to "have a smoke" and cough a bit. He wouldn't have more than one beer in our nightly get acquainted rituals in bars and never found anyone in them worth talking to. He considered the questions people asked about our travels to be nosey invasions of privacy rather than doors to more conversation. He often left the bars early and was usually sitting with a cigarette when I joined him at a motel.

Why did I like his company once a year? It wasn't the riding so much as the kind of bond that simply grows from years of acquaintanceship and the inevitable intimacy of friendship. I still enjoy remembering the nights in motels when we lay on our backs, arms behind our heads in the dark or looking through the smoke from his cigarettes at the ceiling of the motel and laughing about some of our misspent high school and other early years before WWII when we happily worked nights with flirty young waitresses in a restaurant. We jointly owned a Graham Paige convertible automobile—with the rag top missing. We kept it behind the restaurant where we worked and when it wasn't full of water, we'd sometimes take a loaf of cinnamon bread and (selectively) a pair of waitresses to a movie or to Palisades Park after work.

Our most pleasant and most repeated memories were about going to a roller skating rink after work on Friday nights with six or eight waitresses from the restaurant. The head waitress, Ruby, had a '39 Plymouth coupe with a huge trunk, accessible from behind the drivers seat. One or two of the more prudish waitresses would ride next to Ruby up front. The other four or five would lie in the trunk with Sam and me, close as, but more cozy than, cigars in a box. Their husbands and boyfriends were off to WWII camps and battlefields. All of us were young. The girls were between 20 and 30 years old and we were 16 to 18…The girls were lonesome. The songs of the time were all romantic. Under the circumstances, and the influence of the songs, it was a very exciting experience for Sam and me as they played with us in Ruby's trunk. Kissing and feeling were very big in those days. We experienced some wondrous wonders. Some of the girls didn't even bother to skate when we got to the rink. They just sat outside smoking and waiting for the return trip.

Sam and I parted when we both went into the Navy in WWII, but when we came home in 1946; Sam married two of those waitresses, one for three glorious months and the second for the rest of his life.

Sam died in 2003. He hadn't been on a bike for 30 years.

MY SON JOHN

My son, John, accompanied me on many trips in the 1970's and '80's. We share many of the memories mentioned in this book—and others too numerous to mention. The ones I've left out were mostly related to the smaller motorcycles we owned and shorter trips we made in the early years. And we have always spent time together at home with repairs and modifications. John rode with Sam and me on annual trips in the 1970s from the time he was 16 until he had children of his own. I still remember his young frame riding at 50 to 60 mph, usually ahead of me. And then there is my favorite memory—The Race to the Hook.

THE RACE

This favorite memory is about something my son and I repeated many times. It's about when we rode over the Port Jervis Mountain and into the Catskills on the way to my parent's farm seven miles beyond Andes, New York. After a fairly long trip from near Virginia, we would pause in the little town of Andes where a left turn would take us from the small country roads we had traveled to cross over the last mountain and onto a smooth and flat two-lane blacktop, (Route 28) that runs from Andes through a beautiful valley to Delhi, NY.

We would sit at that turn in Andes to adjust our goggles and chin straps, fidget a little—until one of us started our yearly race through the valley for the last seven miles from Andes to the farm—as fast as the motorcycles would go. The best I remember, our top speeds were in the range of 95 to 110 miles an hour, depending on which motorcycles we had at the time.

We made that trip so many times that in later years we didn't stop fully in Andes. Our speeds picked up a little as we passed the Andes cemetery, before we got to the turn, and we jockeyed for the lead position. We just swung around that left turn, neck-to-neck to start the race with an indescribable mixture of excitement, affection and joie de vivre.

We both love that part of the country and especially my parent's small farm, its hundred-plus year old house and barn, the eastern branch of the Delaware River that runs through the property and the small stream in the woods behind the house where my dad sometimes caught trout for breakfast.

Even as I write this thirty years later, I can feel the emotions of those races once again.

A FISHERMAN'S LOOP
A fisherman

In those years we were frequently lost. Now for me, there's a difference between being "lost" and not knowing where you are. Being "lost" involves some feelings of anxiety, but just not knowing where you are isn't all that bad.

John and I often turned into any attractive road that whoever was in the lead might select. I remember a day we were trying to follow a stream that seemed to dodge away from every road we took to follow it. On this day, after we thought we lost the stream, without getting a swim, we were bumping along a dirt road and came to a bridge that crossed over the stream we had just lost! But we felt we had enough of wandering and since there was a guy fishing from the bridge, we asked directions to any main road. He mumbled some guidance without turning to talk and we followed his directions carefully for about twenty minutes and wound up back on the same bridge. The fisherman just looked over his shoulder at us, and for some reason he smiled, as we passed him without stopping to get new instructions. We smiled too, because we weren't lost. We just didn't know where we were. (We should have been suspicious when all the turns he had recommended were right hand turns.)

SMALL GAS TANKS

John often ran out of gas. He had a Harley Sportster with a small gas tank. And when wandering around the Adirondacks, rural Canada and Nova Scotia, there aren't many gas stations. My BMW had a large tank and we occasionally had to use empty beer cans or bottles to drain some gas from my tank for a transfusion to the Sportster. But this only helped for a few miles before we had to stop and do it again. So we started carrying a piece of gas line hose so we could roll his cycle into a ditch to get the height difference needed to siphon gas from the BMW sitting up on the road, directly into the Sportster's tank.

Not many motorcycles had gas gages in the 1960s and '70s. The tanks had fuel spigots that let out gas until they were down to about a gallon. Then the engine would lose speed and cough a little to notify us that we had to go on "Reserve" where the fuel spigot was turned to release that last gallon. It was sometimes dangerous when at high speeds we had to grope around down between our knees to find that fuel spigot while the bike was coughing for gas. And yes, I know—the early Volkswagen Beetles had this same feature

ANOTHER TROUBLE WITH HARLEYS

Everyone wishes he or she could afford one. John loved his Harley Sportster model (as well as his approximately 100 Harley T-Shirts)—and so did everyone he parked close to. One night we were checking into a Motel in Rome, N.Y. and a couple of Harley riders were sitting outside their room near ours. You could tell they were Harley riders because it said so on the back of their black leather vests their T-shirts, their bandannas, their boots and gloves and probably (I'm guessing) their underwear. One of them advised us, "Thanks for bringing us that machine. It will be mine tonight!" We tried to think he was kidding, but decided to roll the Sportster into our room for the night. (They didn't look twice at my BMW.)

WHISKEY OR GAS

One time I had forgotten to reset my gas reserve switch after the previous refill and I ran out of gas just south of Philadelphia. I found an empty Black Velvet whiskey bottle as I hiked a long way to a gas station and was pouring the gas from the whiskey bottle into my tank when a State Trooper stopped just behind the cycle. He walked up and noted me pouring from the Black Velvet bottle. "Mister, if you put that stuff in your tank, you'll blow up your engine!" After my explanation, he gave me some gas from a small portable tank he carried in his trunk, to help motorists, and wished me a good day.

KITTY HAWK AND MYRTLE BEACH

Over the years I've taken some enjoyable trips with my grandsons. The first was with the older one, an overnighter down the Blue Ridge Parkway with some swimming together in a lake near Lynchburg. Later my son and I took him, the grandson, across N.Y. State. (Remember the Niagara Falls, the State Fair and the rain crash at the gravel chute?) When the younger one got old enough, my son and I took the two of them on our two motorcycles for a long trip down the

Atlantic coast from Ocean City, Maryland down to Myrtle Beach, stopping for swims in the ocean every afternoon and watching the boys play in motel pools in the evenings while we shared our happy hours at the tables beside the pools. Highlights included (A) a genuine lack of interest in Kitty Hawk and (B) some Olympic class records in food consumption. And, of course, there was the night that a pony came into the lobby of our hotel near Chincoteague Island, to see what was going on. John and I offered him a seat at the bar, but the manager said the pony was a dead beat and a moocher. He kicked him out.

NOVA SCOTIA

Nova Scotia—"New Scotland" in Latin, is one of my favorite destinations. I've made four trips there from Virginia. The one I made with my son stands out from the other three in my memory.

We left Virginia on a Friday morning, spent one night in Greenpond, New Jersey and circled west of Boston the next day to catch the overnight ferry from Portland, Maine, to Yarmouth, Nova Scotia…

Awaiting the ferry, we parked the bikes in a small fenced parking corral near the ferry ticket office, and joined about a dozen other motorcyclists in a nearby bar to let the heavy trucks get situated on the ferry before loading the motorcycles in the small spaces left over. The bartender gave us all a signal when it was time to load the motorcycles onboard.

On my earlier trips, I bunked with truck drivers in rooms on the ferry that had double decker bunk beds with no sheets; each just equipped with an army-type blanket. I think we used to pay $8.00 more than the base fare to get a bunk bed.

Now the ferries have private bed rooms and a dining room. (Maybe the old ferries still make runs, but this was the only night run). John and I got a tiny room with two bunk beds with sheets and a sink and a toilet.

At unloading time the next morning, John's battery was dead and we had to locate someone with jumper cables to jump-start it. We got it done in time to get off the ship with a dozen other motorcyclists and a dozen trucks at around 6:00 A.M. in Yarmouth. We all rode north through what's called the Coastal Lowlands on the southern tip of Nova Scotia and we all stopped at the first place we could get breakfast—a Bed and Breakfast place in Shelburne. Over coffee, I got to lecturing to my table about how 35,000 "Loyalists" established this town when the British lifted them out of Boston by sea, to protect them from what would happen to them when Washington drove them, the British, out of Boston in the first major engagement of the revolution. Seeing their wives and girlfriends getting interested in my story, the guys announced that we ought to get rolling, and I didn't get to explain why there are now more Loyalists in southwest Ontario. With only John left, and him too polite to leave, I continued my lecture, but I quit when the roar of a dozen Harley Davidsons taking off, including John's, drowned me out.

The breakfast place was not well-equipped to handle such a big gang, but we all were in a happy mood and didn't mind squeezing in and waiting with the good-natured people who seemed to enjoy serving big breakfasts.

After breakfast we found that the battery on John's Harley had not taken a charge on the ride from Yarmouth to the breakfast place. We jump started it again and started northeast. It was a Sunday morning and the few gas stations we found weren't open. We finally found a guy who referred us to a Yamaha dealer. We rode to the location—I think it was in Liverpool, and the place was closed of course, but nearby we found another guy who knew the proprietor and his home phone number. Hearing our sad story and smelling a tidy profit, he decided to skip church and meet us at his shop.

He was a friendly sort but didn't have a battery that would fit into the Harley's battery carriage. So he welded up a frame to mount the smallest battery he had onto John's bike. The deal cost John over a hundred bucks, which is probably less than a new Harley Battery costs, but the patch job was ugly. So John, being a typical Harley rider, had to restore the original battery mounting framework and buy a proper battery when we got home.

Sporting the "customized" battery mounting frame, we continued on up the east coast on what is called the "Lighthouse Route" toward Halifax. By early afternoon we needed some lunch and found a place with a porch table overlooking a beautiful harbor of tall sailing ships in the scenic little seaport of Lunenburg. Directly in front of where we sat was the famous schooner, "Bluenose II," which is commonly known as Nova Scotia's "Sailing Ambassador." She's a majestic 161 feet long according to our post card pictures—with two masts: The main is 126 feet high, the foremast is 118. She's absolutely beautiful, a magnificent tribute to the fishing history of Nova Scotia.

When we were finally able to tear ourselves away from our sunny hour overlooking the Bluenose II, John and I continued northeast to the famous lighthouse at Peggy's Cove. We took some pictures and, looking forward to a lobster dinner, we rode another 30 miles and got a hotel room in Halifax.

On our way northeast to Cape Breton Island the next day, we met pieces of the motorcycle group we had arrived with on the ferry. They, like us, were enjoying the beauty of the country and gobbling up lobster sandwiches at every stopping place along the road. Nobody in Nova Scotia lives more than 50 miles from the sea and the shore line is crowded with neat old fishing boats. After a night sharing our whiskey and telling motorcycle stories in a Cape Breton B&B, we woke up the cat sleeping on John's motorcycle seat and took a 200 mile morning ride around the northeast corner of the Island on the famous Cabot Trail. At rest stops we enjoyed joining other tourists at "scenic view" sites for some whale watching before heading back down the west coast along the Bay of Fundy (no, we didn't see the 50 foot rise when the tide comes in) to Digby, Nova Scotia. There we stayed in another B&B before taking the ferry across the Bay of Fundy to Saint John, New Brunswick. It was a happy trip because the ferry provided pretty costumed dancing girls for us to enjoy.

DANCERS ON FERRY
FROM DIGBY TO
ST. JOHN

DISCONNECTED IN NEW BRUNSWICK

The sun was bright and hot as we came southwest through New Brunswick. As he often did, John decided to race ahead of me a few miles just so he could enjoy the speed on a beautiful winding road through a densely wooded area. Unfortunately, he ran out of gas, so he coasted to a stop to wait for me to catch up. I was somewhat dreamy with the sun flashing through the trees and across the road so I picked up speed to catch up to him. Since I wasn't searching for him, I unconsciously passed by where he sat on the edge of some roadside woods by his bike, and as time passed I started racing to catch him. An hour or so later I stopped at a gas station to think about what I should do. This was before we carried cell phones. I knew he hadn't crashed and there were no crossroads he might have taken, but I rode back about twenty minutes to see if somehow I got by him and he was now trying to catch me! No such luck!

I returned to the gas station and was at the pumps when I heard the Harley coming at high speed. He had seen me pass him hours before, so he knew I was ahead of him somewhere. Fortunately he saw me at the gas pump and took a quarter mile to slow down enough to make a U-turn.

He explained that he had sat for over an hour after I passed him, and he guessed correctly that I would be tearing up the road to catch him. But he had to wait for help to get gas. Finally, a couple on motorcycles had come along, and had seen that he was stranded. They somehow gave him a gas transfusion. By chance, we got an opportunity to thank that couple properly when we met them again that night at a bar in a motel in Bangor, Maine.

CELL PHONES AND CITIZEN BAND RADIO

This is a good place to talk about Cell Phones and CB radios. If we had them at the time of the New Brunswick caper above, John could have called me as soon as I shot by where he was stranded. In recent years I have carried one, mostly to call home to report on where I am, but I also use it to locate campgrounds or other lodgings without having to check door-to-door. I've already mentioned how I can use the cell phone to get my wife to use the internet to find me a place to camp or get a room—after I tell her roughly where I'm headed.

Before I got a cell phone, I carried a hand-held CB, which plugs into the cigarette lighter on my motorcycle. It was and still is, good for contacting truckers to get guidance or reports on traffic jams ahead, but of course is limited to about a mile in range. I still use it because it doesn't require phone numbers to get local advice from the truckers.

When I use these devices, I always think about the fact that wherever I am, I am immersed in an ocean of radio waves. Broadcasts from all the world and signals from satellites, police radios, ham operators—and of course thousands of cell phones—are packed in the air around me, waiting for me to simply pick one for communication, navigation or other computer related things…It's suffocating. I speed up, but they all come with me.

A STREET PARTY IN NEW BRUNSWICK

I haven't always gotten lost in New Brunswick.

Years ago, my wife and I met a friendly couple from New Brunswick while we were on a Caribbean cruise. After a week of hearing my motorcycle stories, they said goodbye with the usual, "Be sure to stop over with us if you ever get to New Brunswick." So, of course, I did.

My wife called the couple from Virginia to tell them I was coming through New Brunswick on a return from Nova Scotia trip. When I got to their house I found they had arranged a "street party." They said it was in my honor—but I have a hunch it was a regular Friday night ritual. But they did hang a few balloons and a "Welcome, Bill" sign. They closed off their street and, with about a dozen neighbors, set up a couple of charcoal burners and tapped a keg of beer! It was as if I had just come "home" from the wars.

Like most Canadians I've met, the people on this block really enjoyed a party. The neighbors had been primed with stories about my travels and I spent a fun summer evening giving their kids rides on the motorcycle and chatting with their parents, some of whom had never been outside of New Brunswick (and couldn't think of any reason they should want to go.).

A couple of telephone calls from some of them to Marilyn, back home in Virginia, and a good night's sleep with a country breakfast was part of the package.

ADVICE TO A SON—THE EIGHT COMMANDMENTS

My long trips with John ended several years ago when he bought a twenty—plus thousand dollar Harley Davidson for he and his wife to make week end trips on. He no longer can get away from work for weeks at a time and his boys, my grandsons, have their own families now. One of them has a new Harley. Here are some of the basic rules I've passed on to them:

- Practice handstands so that when you crash you can use a handstand to go over the handlebars instead of belly first into the handlebars and speedometer.

- Go to bars that have stools rather than booths or chairs. That's so you can stay in the same frozen stance you had for the previous hours on the bike.

- It's hard to look macho when dismounting after a long ride. Try to stop near a wall if possible so you can lean the bike against it instead of making an awkward dismount. If you have to stall until nobody is looking, stay on the bike and cup your hands over you mouth like you are lighting a cigarette.

- Don't even think about toilets once you're in the sleeping bag.

- Remember how the film "Easy Rider" ended when you are considering giving some guy who cuts you off the one finger salute.

- If possible, ride with guys whose gas tanks are bigger than yours.

- Don't lust for what you see riding behind Harley drivers, no matter how tightly her clothes fit.

- Honor thy mother—and don't try to explain your father to her.

OTHER COMPANIONS

I have one more story about traveling with a companion. On a trip I made with a friend from work, Phil Walcoff, the guy you'll hear about in the "Mail Box Crash" in Chapter twelve, we had a humorous experience. We had taken shelter from a rain storm in a hotel in Lynchburg, Virginia, and were enjoying a conversation at the hotel bar when the storm caused a power failure and the hotel lights went out. As part of our conversation with others at the bar, I had explained that we were electricians, so while we all sat in the dark, the lady bartender called the front desk and advised them that she had two electricians at the bar who might be able to help.

The manager soon showed up at the bar with a flashlight and asked if we could do anything. He didn't know whether the whole town had lost power or just the hotel. I asked him to take us to the electric service box where the main circuit breakers are located. While we were approached the box, in the basement, the power came back on without us doing anything.

We returned to the bar to receive cheers and clapping and the manager treated us for a round of drinks—for the entire good natured half dozen of us at the bar. Hoping for a free night's stay, my friend and I registered for the night—but it didn't work. In the morning we had to pay like everyone else.

I should point out that I am quite comfortable in my role as an electrician. I worked as one all through college and in summer breaks from college and I am still wiring houses in the Habitat for Humanity program. And on my summer trips that include stops to visit relatives and old friends, I am often greeted with a list of electrical "projects" that have been held for my arrival.

7

ABOUT MOTORCYCLES

I have made a promise to each of the motorcycles I've owned, that I would forsake all others and be true to it forever. Only my Harley objected to this pledge. (I think it felt that such pledges had connotations of femininity.) To irritate me it vibrated severely when ridden, often lost control of its ignition points and leaked oil in stressful situations. These strike me as definite masculine traits. Riders should be sensitive to this aspect of analyzing the behavior of their machines.

WHAT IS A MOTORCYCLE

The popular reference to motorcycles as "Freedom Machines" seems to capture the sense of escape from the normal stresses of life that riding one can give. But the experience is more complicated than that. Before we talk about some differences in the various machines, there are some factors that are more fundamental than the feeling of "escape."

Think of yourself riding in a convertible car with no floor, no doors and no seat belts. That's scary enough, but now lift the whole car body up and away from the frame…You're still running at 60 mph in a seat which is mounted on some steel piping, but the seat has no back. You're riding a skeleton! Foot brakes won't stop the thing without a separate squeeze from a hand brake, like on your bicycle. And you are looking down where the pavement is flying by just a foot under your feet. Now remember that you can't just turn or even swerve to the right or left. You have to lean into turns. And they call this "escape" from normal anxieties!

You now begin to sense being either too hot or too cold, and the wind bringing in the wonderful fresh air, is mixing it with what my kids call "the wonderful zoo smell" of the farms, pastures and barns you never noticed when driving your car.

Do keep in mind that you have only two wheels, not four. Think of it as having a saddle on a can of gas on top of a powerful engine.

Fortunately it's more comfortable being on one than it is thinking about what it is.

CHANGING MOTORCYCLES

I've enjoyed quite a few different motorcycles over the years. Since 1960 I have owned twelve. Before my present Honda GoldWing, I have had two Binellis, five Hondas, a Yamaha, and two BMWs, an of course a Harley Davidson Superglide in 1971, arguably the most "macho" machine ever.

Sometime in 1976 I got sensible. I realized that for the kind of long trips I was taking, the Harley macho machine was not quite the right bike. Although it generated a kind of respect, tempered with a touch of fear, it was noisy, vibrated for the fun of it and leaked oil. It was better suited for traveling with other Harleys than for going alone into the wilderness. Today all its faults are gone. Now it's just overpriced.

In some ways a new bike is like a new wife; lots of excitement accompanied by lots of readjustment.

Changing from a long relationship with a BMW to anything else requires major mental adjustments. A BMW was, and I believe the air-cooled models still are, the easiest to maintain motorcycles ever made. I rode a BMW R90 for years. But in 1982, I started noticing that Honda GoldWings were silently creeping by me on the highway. The GoldWing was a kind of breakthrough with its four cylinders, smooth and quiet power. Of course there had been four cylinder motorcycles many years ago, most notably the 1919 Hendersons, the 1923 Ace Fours and the 1927 Indian. But the magnificent 1981 Honda GoldWing package brought the four cylinder engines to a new standard for fours in that they were relatively compact, chrome covered, and water cooled.

Before water-cooled engines, the BMW was famous for its lack of vibration. The cylinders were mounted horizontally, one on each side of the bike. Both pistons moved away from, and back toward, the bike at the same time; one on its power stroke while the other was on its exhaust stroke. This balanced movement kept vibration remarkably low. No other engine has this balancing feature. Two, three and four cylinder engines all need counter balancing weights to reduce vibration, but with the four piston cycles per revolution, the vibrations are so close together that they meld into a smooth and pleasant hum, almost like an electric motor hums. At about 60 mph, the "hummmm..." of the engine is like a soft chord on a Cello.

Now while we're this far into it, I should mention that the "V" Twin Harley configuration is really tough to balance out. But "V" enthusiasts would rather live with the balancing weights on the crankshaft than give up the famous "rum-dee-dum" Harley sound at start up and low speeds…You can think of a flywheel that gets two closely spaced pushes and then coasts the rest of the way through each revolution. The sound is addictive and many Harley owners replace the original equipment exhaust systems with the almost straight feed through (no muffler) pipes. They are loud and often illegal, but few states are strict about it.

The GoldWing is not as easy to maintain as the BMW and is heavier due to the four cylinder engine and the water and radiator for water cooling. The BMW, until recently, had a seat shaped like a large banana with the tips cut off…It made the rider restless after a few hours of riding. As you slipped slowly forward, your jockey shorts got tighter. The handlebar location made the rider lean slightly forward. I think the German's, who only travel at maximum speed, believed this hunched over position would lower wind resistance and that air slamming into the bent-forward chest and stomach might even provide a bit of "lift" to reduce the rider's weight on the handlebars and on the seat, thus allowing the riders under shorts to loosen up. (Assuming speeds of over a hundred miles an hour.) Many American riders, including me, replaced the BMW's small handlebars with bigger ones and replaced the seats to allow us to sit vertically, like police bikes do, for a more comfortable ride. In fact, for very long trips, both my son and I used to use pillows on the banana shaped seats of his Sportster and my early BMW.

My GoldWing has a broad seat like you used to see on old Indian cycles (shaped like an upholstered farm tractor seat) and detachable luggage suitcases. It has been ideal for my type of cruising. Most of the current built-for-cruising motorcycles have all these features, but they are usually covered under streamlined fiberglass. To my taste the new ones look more like gondolas than motorcycles. Mine was built before engines got concealed in plastic. I am with the Harley Davidson riders on this. We see these engines as works of art, to be left uncovered so they can be seen. Fortunately there are enough of us, especially Harley riders, to influence the Japanese copiers to build a line of engines that look like Harleys. But the majority of their sales to adults are big bikes with everything associated with the engine hidden under plastic. Just like an automobile.

CHAOS INSIDE AN ENGINE

When cruising along alone on a highway with no particular ideas to occupy my mind, I enjoy the soothing purr of my engine. On an especially hot day on a hot highway, I sometimes get concerned about how the engine must feel about the heat. I get thinking about what Joan of Arc said at the stake as they lit the fire ("I hate it when they do that!") The Chicago fire of 1871 also comes to mind. So does the movie, "Towering Inferno." I hate for the engine to have to run in this heat! I worry about its pulse and blood pressure.

The motorcycle instruments read 65 mph at 4000 rpm. Golly! This engine is turning around 67 times every second! 67 TIMES EVERY DAMNED SEC-OND! That alone is enough to make a sensible person nervous. It means that each piston is changing direction 134 times a second! And those dear little points are being pushed apart 33 times every blessed second! It's no wonder the fiber "point-pusher" wears down. Even those perfectly adjusted valves are each changing direction 66 times a second. I've tried wiggling my finger that fast. I've also tried to silently count to 33 in a second and got to about 10.

Going further, in each of those 67 per second revolutions, each of my four cylinders must move down about 2.5 inches, stop and move back up 2.5 inches. So, they each move 5 inches 67 times a second, or 1675 feet every minute. With 5280 feet in a mile, my four cylinders are each traveling just under a third of a mile a minute, half in one direction and half in the opposite direction, at roughly 20 miles an hour, as they reverse direction 67 times a second!

Even if you don't want to check my arithmetic, you've got to wonder how the thing can run smoothly when the piston is reversing direction 67 times a second. The answer must be that, as I've said before, everything is moving so damned fast that the machine doesn't have time to vibrate!

Not even an astronaut would risk his or her life on a thing that relies on so many parts moving so fast. But we motorcyclists aren't very logical. We don't want to be forced to conclude that we really should quit motorcycling.

And all this action goes on for hours at a time! Right under my seat! In all this heat! I can't get over how fantastic it is. Sometimes, overcome with emotion, I determine to start a new religion, (non-profit and tax-exempt of course)—a cult of motorcycle worshippers. It couldn't be any dumber than most of the other cults we read about. As long as I'm riding on a dull road, let's pause and think about that.

STARTING ANOTHER RELIGION

A new motorcycle cult! What an interesting idea it seemed to be as the sun beat down on my black helmet and the highway started getting wavy in the distance. Let's think this through. Firstly, would the IRS allow my expenses to travel and talk to old engine lovers? Could I collect dues from my worshipful followers? Like any cult worth its salt, my new religion would have to have something to be against. For openers, let's be against recapped truck tires that peel off on hot roads.

Yeah! I hate them! (In coal country, I think they are specially designed to drop big pieces off every 50 yards—and they can't be removed for at least a year.) We'll talk more about them when we get to "near accidents" in Chapter X. Right now I'm imagining my first sermon for the new religion. Citing the experiences of other motorcyclists and some claims that the Federal Government is not giving adequate attention to this problem because of the power of the Trucker's lobby, I think I could work myself and my people into a real hysterical, foot stompin' rage—like other fanatics do! Maybe I can associate recapped tires as precursors of the "second coming!" (Recapped tires after all are like a second coming for tires.) They are easy to hate, not only dangerous, but downright ugly! And trucks are dropping them every fifty yards all over the country! Let's lock up the truck drivers who drop them. After listening to that O.J. trial stuff for so long on TV, I feel we've just got to jail somebody.

A NEW MACHINE.

After nearly 20 years of trips on my 1976 BMW R90/6, I felt some version of guilty when I left home on a replacement. But she was getting past middle age and no longer had the shapeliness, firmness and youthfulness of the younger ones. In my garage, with the GoldWing packed to leave, I felt more comfortable pushing the new machine around the side of my car opposite from where the BMW stood. An old divorce dirge flashed across my mind, "I gave you the best years of my life and now you…" etc.

On the day I planned to depart, it rained. Unlike my always-ready-to-go BMW, the Honda called for a two day delay beyond my planned departure. After all, she was young and her beautiful body not yet touched by the vicissitudes of life on the road—so I waited for the rains to pass.

Although I try to minimize my time on major highways, I wanted to make a high speed run with the new machine. The super highway from my home area with the least traffic and best farm country views is Interstate 81 South. And so it was that on a hot July day I headed for the Blue Ridge to join 81 at Lexington, Virginia.

I headed south to Charlottesville and west toward the Blue Ridge Mountains at Rockfish Gap. The machine seemed to enjoy this first hour as much as I did as I ran with the joy of having something new and powerful to enjoy on a sunny day. The fresh air and the quiet sounds of nature along the country roads seemed to be amplified by their contrast with the quietness of the engine.

FIRST IMPRESSIONS

After an hour riding on the new Honda, the stirrings of a routine matter began to disturb me. It was my habit of eating breakfast. The old BMW would have been at home pulling into the little town of Stuarts Draft where I had breakfasted so many times in the past. As mentioned earlier, I like to ride an hour or two before breakfast and going south, Stuarts Draft has the first mom-and-pop place that's the right distance from home. Here the local retirees meet and the construction guys get their Thermos coffee refills, and it feels good when the counter girl says, "Hey! Where 'yuh been?"

Belly full and anxious to continue my trip, I eased onto Interstate 81 South at Lexington to see how the Honda behaved at high speeds. She felt like she loved it and wanted to stay on 81. I was pleased with this and sensed that significant bonding had begun. I mused on how an hour or so at seventy some miles an hour bonds the rider to the bike. It's hard to explain. Maybe it's the sense of trust that the machine can and will perform as you want it to. And, some of us add a sense of appreciation for the magnificence of the engines now being built. Speed alone seems to contribute to the "feeling of freedom" syndrome. Anyway, it feels good.

All day the names of the towns and places I passed made me smile: Rockfish Gap, Stuarts Draft, Greenville, Steeles Tavern, Vesuvius, Fancy Gap, Twin Oaks, Deep Gap, Cranberry, and Natural Bridge. Although pleased with the high speed performance of the machine, eventually I needed to cool down. So I got off hot 81 at Buchanan to climb up 4,000 feet to the cooler Blue Ridge Parkway at the Peaks of Otter. Cooler air enfolded me and the Honda, and crept inside my helmet to deal with my hair, so wet from sweat. This, plus the magnificent views, helped me forget about the heat. The Parkway bypassed Roanoke and provided postcard views of well-groomed farms and small towns in the valleys on both sides of the mountain.

It was late in the afternoon when I had to drop down off the Parkway for gas, to a little town called Floyd. With a cold Gatorade, I sat by the gas pumps next to a guy who had been admiring the GoldWing. He was just telling me how he wished he could take off cross-country when we heard threatening thunder and saw the flash of heat lightning to the south. My instincts suggested that this storm was trying to tell me to go back home. They were right, but I ignored them. But I at least got the message that I couldn't make it to Asheville.

THE TRUCKER'S POINT OF VIEW

I was now hot and sweaty again. With storms ahead, my gas station friend recommended 50 miles of country road to Mount Airy, North Carolina, where I checked into a motel with a pool. It was next to a truck stop. The thunderstorm had stayed southwest of us, and the temperature was still near 90 degrees. I got a cold six-pack in the truck stop and joined a couple of truckers at poolside, picking a seat where my eyes could fondle my new motorcycle. We split the beers while they explained to me why cars, pick-ups and motorcycles shouldn't be allowed on the roads, because roads are for trucks!

Although this was a good framework for an argument, due to my forgiving nature when dealing with men bigger than me, I forced a smile and joined them for spaghetti and chicken livers. We all enjoyed our waitress.

"Be right with you, Honey."

"What can I get you, Darlin'?"

"Anything else, Sweetheart?"

It's no wonder the truckers stop for gas so often.

I went to bed thinking about the day on the new machine, fretting about the weather and wondering if the waitress would still call me "Darlin'" in the morning.

I got up early and opened the drapes to a sunny morning. After jumping in the pool for a few minutes, I hit the lobby for free coffee, after which I dried off heavy dew from the seat of the Honda with a motel towel and checked my maps. The rain seemed to have passed and no dark clouds were in sight as I rode a sunny hundred miles along the Yadkin River through Wilkesboro, Lenoir and Morganton before breakfast.

My chosen road was "Closed for Construction" below Lenoir, but no one was policing it. To avoid a long detour, I went around the "Closed" sign and proceeded along a recently cleared construction road. The guys and girls who were supposed to hold Stop and Go signs to get the construction trucks through the one-way sections, just sat by the roadside drinking their morning coffee and nodding to me as I wobbled through. Road clearance on the Honda was barely adequate on the rough construction roads which were full of ditches, tire tracks and pools of rain water, none of which would have bothered the BMW, which had better road clearance.

Some gray clouds snuck in while I ate breakfast in Morganton, and a light rain pestered me as I approached Asheville through the mountains on Route 40 around noon. Thunderheads appeared over the mountains ahead and they challenged me to a race to a cabin on a mountain.

8

CABINS, FARMS AND MOUNTAINS

MY THIRD CABIN

Doug and Becky Snure lived in a cabin up a winding, one-lane dirt road on a mountain in Canton, N.C...Doug is a retired Honeywell executive. Until recently they lived for several years wandering around the Caribbean and the south Pacific in their floating home, a Crealock 37 sailing yacht they named "Odyssey." Taking a break from that life at sea after crossing the Pacific to New Zealand, they were now building a cabin in the mountains. Earlier that year I spent a couple of weeks doing the electrical work as they and their contractors built it. Having traveling with them on their boat for a couple of short periods in the Caribbean and on the Intercoastal Waterway, I was now anxious to see them again and see how they adapted to life in a remote cabin in the mountains after sailing full time around so much of the world for so many years.

Dark skies and lightning were a few miles in front of me as I left Highway 40 on a rural road in Canton to climb their mountain. The rain started and when I saw that the storm had me beat, my eyes searched through wet and fuzzy goggles for an open barn or shed to pull into. Turning off the hard road, I started up the single lane dirt road that was cut into the side of the mountain with no shoulders. On my left side, the mountain dropped steeply down and on my right the mountain slope went up like a steep dirt wall. When the tires on the heavy motorcycle began losing traction in the mud, I got very anxious about the sharp drop on the left. The sky was now black and between the flashes of lightning my headlight gave me a fuzzy view through rain speckled goggles into the tunnel of trees and bushes soaking down to enclose the muddy road ahead.

Because the heavily loaded Honda was fishtailing as she climbed through the mud, I needed both hands on the handlebars, but still couldn't steady her enough to snatch my sunglasses off and get them into a pocket. They just added to the storm's darkness and I was afraid to stop to do something about it for fear of not being able to get traction to start uphill again.

The rain now felt like I was riding through a waterfall. With the big machine there was no room to turn around and get back down to the hard roads. As I finally slipped around the last hairpin turn below their cabin, the trees parted around their cleared parcel of land and there was enough light for me to see the cabin. Their entrance was on the uphill side of their parcel and I turned right without stopping when I rounded the last hairpin turn and got to it. I wobbled down their dirt driveway—aiming the machine at their open garage doors.

Unfortunately there was a mound of soft sand, now mud, piled across the garage entrance, waiting to be part of the cement for a ramp up from the driveway onto the garage floor. I tried to ram the Honda through it into the garage, but sunk into it up to my wheel hubs. Both wheels! The exhausted Honda stood there looking pathetic in the rain while it's exhausted rider struggled off and slogged into the garage.

My friends in the cabin did not see this grand entrance. They were staining the inside log walls and negotiating things with some of their construction guys upstairs. They were under roof and paid no mind to the occasional summer thunderstorms one lives with in the mountains. A half hour after I got there, the summer sun was out! It took three of us to get the motorcycle out of the mud and into the garage.

I spent that afternoon and next day wiring a well pump and an electric floor heater that had not been available on my last visit,—and lacing up some final wiring and telephone connections at the Service breaker box. I enjoy this kind of work (when it's raining outside) and after dinner we updated news about our families and recalled good times together.

Life on the mountain seemed to agree with my friends. Having lived so long on a boat, they were tuned to appreciating every aspect of their mountain environment. They obviously enjoyed a degree of separation that only a few people experience today. They enjoy cooking, reading, gardening and, most of all, the beauty of the view across the blue-gray Smoky Mountains they overlook from their cabin. They enjoy visits of the many friends they have made traveling. Doug has installed and stocked a wine cooler, so they always have the right wine to complement their gourmet cooking. Satellite TV provided them with hundreds of views of life around the country and the world, and if any of this stimulated their interest, they left the mountain to travel awhile. Except for their travel option, and their ability to buy whatever they want, they have a lot in common with most mountain people, feeling the almost holy respect and affection for the beauty of their environment.

DOWN ONE MOUNTAIN AND UP ANOTHER

The dirty bike and I departed on a sunny morning to cruise along the south edge of the Smoky Mountains, where the campgrounds, motels and restaurants in Maggie Valley, Cherokee and Bryson City were bulging with happy families on summer vacation, all dressed in bright colors, maybe hoping gaudy clothes would keep the Indians at bay.

I wangled a visitors pass for "The Prettiest Park in the Smokies," run by The Cherokee Nation. There I enjoyed a swim and had lunch in the clubhouse, surrounded by mountains rising from a rushing stream or small river, that ran into a clear lake, in the "Happy Holiday RV Park and Campground". It has over 300 campsites, cabins and bunkhouses and if I hadn't made a date for the night further down in Robbinsville, I'd have set up my tent there and taken a rafting trip on the nearby Nantahala River. Instead, I went on, traveling beside the river and looking down on it from the road at hundreds of rafters from dozens of spots along the river road. I made a mental note—to come back.

A FARM IN THE MOUNTAINS

At the southern end of the Smoky Mountains, Kathy and Jim Denton, own a farm and several hundred acres of trees on Snowbird Mountain, above Robbinsville, North Carolina. Their place is so hard to get to, with so many intersecting dirt roads, that I arranged to meet Jim at a Hardees restaurant in Robbinsville, thinking to follow him up the mountain to their farm. But having had that recent experience with the rain on the mountain road to the cabin, I hurried to get to Hardees ahead of Jim, so I could ride around the area and look for an elderly couple sitting on a porch or in their yard. I found Mr. and Mrs. Wayne Carringer, told them my hope to leave the bike in the village and ride up the mountain in Jim's truck...I offered them $20 a night to let me leave the motorcycle behind their house. They said sure, I could leave the bike, but, "We wouldn't take money for what we consider normal hospitality." We exchanged stories about "where yuh' from," our families and Snowbird Mountain before I parked the machine under a back porch overhang behind their house, grabbed some skivvies from my saddle bags, and jogged back to Hardees—free to ride up the mountain in Denton's truck

Jim was there at Hardees when I arrived and we took off in his truck. He had to get out of the truck to unlock a couple of gates along "Little Snowbird Road," before we visited a small clearing in the woods where several generations of Dentons are buried. Jim's family had retrieved a couple of gravestones and bodies from military cemeteries where his dad and uncles had been buried. They brought the men home to Snowbird and used the military headstones as bench tops on granite legs by the graves! It was a touching and somehow beautiful experience to visit this quiet place in the mountains where generations of one family rested on their own land, in a small cleared area in the dense woods.

Approaching the Denton farm, a dozen or so cows came across the fields to meet Jim's truck and asked what he had brought for them this time. Jim's wife, Kathy, calls them "Jimmy's girls" because he's so fond of them.

The old family house sits on a small semi-circular plateau that juts out from one of the mountains that rise sharply on all sides of the farm. The plateau is about 50 yards in diameter and has a line of magnificent old trees lined along its edge. From the porch of the house, or from a hammock between two of the trees, one looks down on the pasture, about 50 feet below. The only sounds are from the cows below and a gurgling mountain stream tumbling down the mountain behind the house, and on down where the pasture catches and guides it along an assortment of barns, sheds and fencing that speckle its banks before it reaches the edge of the steep mountains that define the pasture's boundaries.

We spent a memorable evening on the porch with our feet up on the handrails, talking about the past, swatting an occasional fly and sipping some special local whiskey supplied by another local mountain man.

You won't believe what all we did the next day. And if you are not interested in what goes on in the mountains, you should skip to where I get back on the motorcycle a few pages hence—where it says DEALS GAP. (But remember I told you in the Introduction that one of the three ways I get to know people is to take on jobs they need to have done.)

THE LOGGING BUSINESS

My first lesson was in the basics of logging. It started when we were drinking early morning coffee and the quietness was broken by the arrival of heavy diesel machinery a short way up the mountain behind the house. A man named John Moody was up there with his Bulldozer pushing 16-foot tree trunks along the ground to where his son, Marti, sat waiting 12 feet off the ground on their "Knuckle Boom Log Loader"—a monster mechanical dinosaur with huge jaws that can reach out 20 feet and hoist gigantic logs onto their huge and well worn flatbed truck. Nearby stood a backhoe they need to clear brush for a logging road and a clear place to work in the woods. John and his son, and the four big diesels, have been logging all their lives, much of it on Denton's Mountain, called "Snowbird" on the maps, where they share their earnings with the Dentons as a way of paying for the lumber.

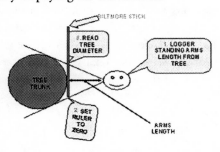

MEASURING TREE DIAMETER USING BILTMORE STICK

John showed me how he uses a "Biltmore Log Scale" to estimate the number of board feet he can get from a tree. The scale looks like a yard stick, but is calibrated to measure log diameter and the number of 16-foot "logs" in the height of the tree. These two measures then determine the number of board feet he can get from the trees.

Here's how it works. He holds the stick horizontally against the tree and stands back at arm's length, 25 inches, from it. He moves the stick horizontally to line up its zero (left) end with the left edge of the tree. Without moving his head or the stick, he looks to the right to read what the stick measures to the right edge of the tree. The stick is calibrated to read diameter directly. (It's not like moving your head over to measure the diameter directly from a yard stick because your answer would depend on knowing exactly how far to move. Besides, these trees are a lot bigger than one-yard stick could measure.)

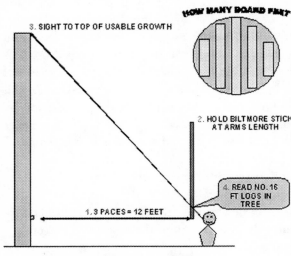

HOW MANY 16 FT. LOGS IN A TREE

The procedure is similar for measuring height. The logger stands 12 paces from the tree, sights the bottom of the vertical stick's zero at his own height and looks at what the stick reads at the point on it that lines up with the top of the usable height of the tree. The stick converts each 16-foot log to usable board feet. A 16-feet log that is 16 inches in diameter yields 181 board feet using this stick. It even allows ¼ in. waste on each cut for the saw blade thickness! In these particular mountains where much of the lumber used to come from Biltmore family property, the "Biltmore Stick", is still used. (How the Biltmore stick is calibrated is explained on the web.)

When I was there, loggers were getting around $245 for a thousand feet of #3 grade pine or $500 per thousand for veneer grade poplar. So if John and Marti haul out a truckload of ten 16 footers at 181 board feet each, that's 1810 board feet, or $500-$750 (if one is veneer grade) for a day's work. That is for two men, a lot of equipment, and a significant fraction to the tree owner. That's Jimmy.

THE ROMAN AQUEDUCT

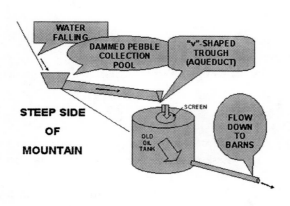

Our first "chore" after our chat with the loggers was to fix a broken water system that was supposed to capture the clear cold water running down the mountain above the house and delivered it to a couple of places near the barns and sheds. The source was up on the mountain where the stream took a steep drop down over some rocks. Jim had made a V-shaped wooden trough, about four inches wide, to drain water from a very small pool he made in the falling water's path above a section with a steep drop. The trough feeds water from the small pool, out almost horizontally like a Roman viaduct to the top of a five-foot high, rusty old cylindrical tank that used to store oil for some one's oil burner. The home-made "viaduct" is held up at the top by rocks around the little pool's edge, and by rickety wooden stilts as it gently slopes down about eight feet to the tank. The trough is old and lined with green moss, but it rushes wonderfully clear drinking water into the top of the tank.

Everything is leaking or over flowing with the wonderful water, including the pool, the trough and the tank. But who cares!

A screen on top of the tank blocks small stones, twigs, leaves, nuts from entering the three-foot-diameter tank. About a foot from the bottom of the tank, a three inch pipe feeds the water through a PVC pipe on down to the farm. Access to the inside bottom of the tank to clean out any sediment used to be through a

12-inch square opening on one side, but the studs to hold the hole's cover on were rusted away. So our job was simply to rig a belt around the tank, tight enough to hold the cover on, (still happily leaking water all around its edges) and to replace some of the downstream pipe that had been broken when the logging road was put in.

We drank the cold and somehow delicious mountain water like it was a reward for our work, as it gushed out of a pipe down by the farm's sheds. Jim had a faucet like valve in the line rigged to a fire hose, always ready for use. From these outlets, the water drops another two feet back into the streambed and rushes on across the pasture. It's a wonderful set up.

SNAKES IN THE GRASS

Next we had to walk around the pasture to pick up pieces of a tin roof that a recent storm had blown off one of the sheds. I was about to pick up one piece that lay out in the sun when Jim said "Don't pick up that one. There's sure to be a snake under it." I picked up the piece anyway, and sure enough; a three-foot long snake scurried out from under it. Jim pointed out that it was only good luck he didn't scurry my way, not knowing what threat he was facing. I'm not sure what kind of snake it was, but I learned that the Denton family is on constant alert for poisonous snakes on the farm, especially in the pasture and in the sheds.

FIXING FARM MACHINERY

Jim doesn't have a barn, but he has four or five sheds lined along a dirt and grass roadway beside the stream that comes down from where we repaired the "aqueduct" and runs through the property. Actually it's one long shed, wide open on one side, but kind of divided into 8 foot sections between the poles that support the common tin roof. Each section is outfitted like a separate shed; one for the big tractor, another for mowing equipment, etc.

The section I liked best was probably the most disorganized. Like my father's old barn in upper New York State, this shed is full of very old tools, hardware and mechanical mysteries, on a dozen shelves that dated back to the 1930s. Open jars full of screws, nuts, bolts, washers and so forth, are topped off with insect nests, squirrel nuts, spider webs and strange hay-like stuff you can blow away before you pour the hardware into your hands and shake out the rust and broken things to find something.

In another section, one past Jim's bulldozer and backhoe sections, there is a heavy trailer on which he has mounted a motor generator, an air compressor and his welding equipment. Jim uses his tractor to pull this rig anywhere he needs to use his pneumatic and electric tools and or his welder. He also has a motorcycle and a four-wheeler (a saddle mounted on a motorcycle engine slung between four big balloon tires). We rode these to a neighboring farm to see a new "portable" saw mill, i.e. a big round blade driven by a gasoline engine—all mounted on a trailer with big enough tires to pull through rough terrain.

On this day, in one particular shed, there was a sickle-bar disc-mower to repair. This is a tractor attachment that has mechanical arms that stick out about 5 feet on one side of the tractor. Four twirling circular discs with stubby radial blades sticking out of them are mounted side-by-side on the arms. Tractor power is a lot greater than lawn mower motor power and as these rotating blades skid along the ground, they cut almost anything in their way. Anything they can't cut is big enough for the tractor driver to see before they get to it.

As we replaced the dozen or so parts that Jim had special ordered for the sickle bar mower, I quietly imagined how great it would be to hook one up to my motorcycle so I could slash tires on 18-wheelers whenever they crowded me.

A BONFIRE ON A HOT DAY?

I'll skip the parts about "worming" the cows and the inspiring behavior of young bulls in amongst mature lady cows, and I'll jump to the end of the day when Jim's wife and daughter, Hilary, and I were assigned to "pasture cleanup" before dinner. We made a pile of rotted logs, old split rail fencing, branches, dead shrubs and stuff that cluttered the pasture, for a big bonfire. We carried or rolled the stuff to an area where Jim bulldozed it into a pile, covered it with old engine oil and set it afire.

With the fire roaring comfortably, we all retreated from the heat, up to the hammock and chairs under the huge trees on the edge of the plateau on which the house overlooks the pasture, the grazing cows, the stream around the pasture and the mountains rising on all sides to border the beauty and mood set by the scene. As we sat quietly sweating from our efforts, and looked down on the fire in the pasture below the iced tea was like Champaign.

But fast moving black clouds began to appear over one edge of the circle of mountains around the farm and the bonfire's vertical column of black smoke bent down to rush horizontally away from them. Storms seem to arrive suddenly in the mountains because you can't see them coming from afar. Jim and I took our chairs up under the porch overhang and watch the storm come and try once more to cope with his "special" whiskey while Kathy and Hilary got pork chops, corn and tomatoes ready for the outside grill. When we felt adequately fueled, Jim and I did the "stop the rain" dance. It's a hard dance to do. (You have to do the regular rain dance backwards to stop rain.) But it seemed to work. The storm moved fast and on over us following where the black smoke had gone. Jim, being careful to keep his glass of home brew a good distance from the charcoal burner, cooked the chops in a light drizzle. I slept well that night.

It was raining the next morning. Evidently we hadn't done the complete version of the rain dance. Anyway the family had to travel back to their business in Asheville that day. So instead of facing frying pans and dirty dishes, we went down the mountain for breakfast at the Hardees where Jim had picked me up. After breakfast they left and I sat an extra hour looking out the windows at the rain and drinking coffee between trips to the men's room where I could lock myself in the handicapped people's toilet booth and do an abbreviated version of the stop-rain dance.

As soon as the rain eased up I went to retrieve my motorcycle from behind Mr. Carringer's house. It was still raining softly as I rode through a short cut in the Cheoah Mobile Home Park back to Hardees where I could repack my luggage for a rainy trip west.

A dozen or so local regulars were still sitting around at Hardees, mostly at window tables, drinking coffee and telling each other what they had planned to do if it weren't raining. Most of them were construction guys who would leave for work if the rain stopped, but would rather stay here than go home if it didn't stop. Their pick-up trucks, each with its rusting tool box mounted on its back, along with miscellaneous beer or coke cans, MacDonald's wrappings, an unmounted spare tire and some piece of unidentifiable metal in their truck beds—huddled in the rain around my GoldWing as if they were commenting on the wet weather and conversing with the bike about its travels. It was a similar scene inside, where I sat alone with my helmet and a bag or two, drinking coffee and looking at maps, chatting with the truck's drivers.

The usual dialog began in the usual way. From a table behind me, "I use to have a Harley. One of them big 64s." Others offered their motorcycle stories awhile from other tables. They ended when the rain lightened up—with some advice.

"You ought to take 129 up to the famous motorcycle camp at Deals Gap, just north of here."

I did.

DEALS GAP AND THE TAIL OF THE DRAGON

In the light rain, I rode up to the camp as they recommended. It's on the southern end of the Smoky Mountains in North Carolina, near the border with Tennessee, about 25 miles Northwest of Robbinsville, on a section of Route 129.

A big road sign announces you're at Deals Gap, but the facility is called "The Crossroads of Time". It's a combination motel, cabin, campground, souvenir and gas station complex. Its sign says it is a "Motorcycling Paradise."

This stretch of route 129 was once named in Motorcyclist Magazine as, "one of the 10 Best Motorcyclists Roads in America. It has 311 curves in an eleven mile section called "The Dragon's Tail". Riders come from all over the world to try their hand at racing through these curves, probably because all the records are recorded at the Crossroads of Time facility along with pictures of record holders along with artifacts from the many crashes that have occurred there.

Along the winding road there are pieces of motorcycles nailed to trees where bikers have died—some from going off the road into the trees and some from crashes in the two lane roadway.

Attempts to break speed records here are known as attempts to "slay the dragon." There are numerous accidents on the Dragon every week and a couple of deaths almost every year. (Read about it on the Web under either Tail of the Dragon or Deals Gap)

One end of the Dragon starts at The Crossroads of Time. The other end is a place called Tabcat Creek Bridge. I wanted to give my Gold Wing a run on it and evaluate a feature that was bothering me a little. The big four cylinder engine in the Honda, along with the raised luggage compartment on the back, has raised the center of gravity of the machine quite a bit higher than it was on the low slung opposing cylinders of the BMW I had for so many years. It didn't make a difference at cruising speeds but made me a bit nervous leaning into tight turns.

Besides, running the Dragon entitles the rider to wear a special, widely respected amongst cycle riders, "Deals Gap" T-shirt!

The campground manager showed me the central campgrounds recreation room where visiting bikers spend their evenings talking about the Dragon and other adventures they've had. The room has dozens of pictures of motorcyclists who had stayed there with license plates from all over the U.S. and Canada. He showed me books of accident pictures and of super bikers who ended in pieces along the road. He suggested that I get a room and wait for the road to dry before facing the Dragon. But, it was still early in the day and, influenced by the long boring hours at Hardees, I was probably hyped up a bit from approximately ten cups of coffee, I decided to give the Dragon a try.

Winding roads with blind curves make me especially nervous when it's raining, but I started counting the three hundred and eleven curves, wiping the rain from my goggles with one wet glove and trying to steer with the other. Nobody else was on the road, but I still felt anxious facing every curve, about meeting a vehicle coming toward me. I think I was up to about twenty curves when the anxiety got to me and I forgot about counting. It was when I saw the Tennessee River too close on my right, and decided on a U-turn to go back.

I didn't stop at the Crossroads because I was afraid they'd take a picture of "the guy too chicken to complete the Dragon." And I haven't thought about the GoldWing's center of gravity since.

THE SUN SOMETIMES RISES

I was now riding alongside Lake Fontana and it was still raining. I didn't have time to do what Noah did. It takes too long to round up the necessary animals. But my mind did release a dove with instructions to bring me an olive branch. She came back soaking wet—with no olive branch. On her second trip I imagined I saw an olive branch. Maybe I was hallucinating, but I knew that there must be dry land ahead. The third time, she didn't return, so I imagined she must be eating soup in Fontana Village. I got there and downed some hot soup—and sure enough, as my senses recovered from hours of rain, I got a fuzzy vision of her at a nearby table.

I put on some dry underwear in the men's room and hung around the gift shop writing post cards and pricing wooden figures and other crafts, most of which were made in China, until the sun finally crept out. I walked around the village and took a few pictures—still hoping that nobody would recognize me as the motorcyclist who bought the "I Rode the Dragon" Tee shirt at the Crossroads of Time and then didn't finish the ride.

In this, then remote, area, Fontana Village was built at the beginning of WWII to support the men who built the great Fontana Dam. Hydroelectric power was needed to support the secret facilities at Oak Ridge where some aspects of the A-Bomb development were being addressed—aspects that called for a lot of electric power. Today the village, with its inn, cottages and campgrounds, a church, a hospital, a museum, a laundry, post office, craft house, and a school, has evolved to be a popular resort for hiking, fishing, swimming, rafting, tennis, basketball, biking, horseback riding, miniature golf, souvenir shopping and exercising at the fitness center to fill in the time between meals at any of several attractive eateries.

Fontana is near the southern end of the Smoky Mountains. From Fontana Village I went north on still-wet roads to the most popular tourist route into the mountains.

9

THE GREAT SMOKY MOUNTAINS

There are only a few good roads through the Smoky Mountains. Route 441 gets most of the tourist traffic. It goes northwest from the Cherokee Indian Reservation I mentioned earlier, to Gatlinburg, Tennessee. The mountains were extensively logged around the turn of the century and along 441 I saw the remains of old roads, now grown over with greenery, and a few dirt and gravel ones that dead-ended in the woods. The mountain roads had been tidied up under the public works programs of the 1930's when the National Park Service acquired the land. The limited sense of history a visitor gets is from some exhibits in two Visitor Centers.

CADES COVE

The real treat for tourists is up a side road off of 441 that leads to a small plateau in the middle of the mountains—to a place called Cades Cove. Originally an Indian community, the Cove was settled by several dozen Colonial families after the Indians were forced out as part of the "Vale of Tears" transfer to Oklahoma. The Cove is toured on an eleven mile, one-way oval road along which the Park Service has restored the farm and church buildings that were there in the 1800s. The place gives a visitor a real feeling for the bleak lives of the mountain people who once lived there.

The Cove gets over two million visitors a year! I had hoped to set up my tent in the Cades Cove Campground, but once inside the Cove, I found myself in a long line of slow moving cars and campers. With the motorcycle I can wiggle a bit through jagged lines of cars, but it still takes about three hours to visit the sites around the loop, and weaving through a line of slow moving vehicles is never fun. Irritated people feel that you are "jumping the line," and you have to fear they might swing a car door open as you ride closely by. (It's entirely different from the attitude in Germany, Italy, Switzerland and California, where people have grown to accept cycle riders zipping between lines of cars.)

Although I was not able to get a spot in the campground for my tent, I was offered a sleeping space by two couples who shared a spot. They were taking a break from hiking the Appalachian Trail, which crosses 441 not far from the side road to Cades Cove. I enjoyed swapping travel stories with them. They had hiked up the mountain from Lake Fontana and had high praise for the Tennessee Valley Administration program that created the Fontana Dam—and for Roosevelt's program to develop the Appalachian Trail.

Even though they had only hiked a tiny fraction of the famous Georgia to Maine Appalachian Trail, two kinds of things bothered them. One was that the mountain bears were so used to the presence of humans, and their good food, that camping at the Trail's shelters was getting dangerous. The other was that the popularity of the Trail was beginning to make it crowded. The latter was aggravated by Park regulations that forced "clustering" of hikers, which is by requiring people to camp only at shelters.

I have crossed the Appalachian Trail quite a few times in Virginia and New England, and have had many conversations with its devotees, especially when I (often) camped at the Big Meadows campgrounds on the Skyline Drive. Suffice to say, the hikers are a hardy bunch who endure isolation, unpleasant meals, days without hot water, not to mention sore feet and overall weariness—to enjoy being close to nature. (They don't always admit that they drop off the trail every couple of days for the comforts of motels and restaurants.)

CROWDS

Coming down from the mountains, I found the "Sugarlands Visitor Center," two miles before Gatlinburg. It was like Cades Cove, jammed with tourists. It seemed like everyone had to end their day of bumper-to-bumper traffic in the mountains with a pit stop here. Then came the tourist-oriented billboards and neon signs unfolding around our mob as we crept into Gatlinburg. For me it was depressing. From the magnificent glory of the mountains, one enters a dense and gaudy complex of commercial shops and road signs. All of my fellow travelers however behaved cheerfully, as if this was what they had come for.

Maybe I was too impatient. I left without ever giving the famous town a chance. I headed northeast along the Webb, English and Stone Mountain ranges in the northwestern Smokies before stopping at a Visitor's Information Center in

Newport, Tennessee. It was getting on toward evening now and a charming lady at the counter found me a motel to off-load my baggage and put on a dry shirt. There I got a six pack from the gas station across the street to help me get friendly with the motel counter lady and a couple of other guests watching TV in the motel lobby. I asked one of the other guests about visiting nearby Dolly Parton's "Dollywood" amusement park. The group advised against it, and offered that the once quiet town of Pigeon Forge was now a mess of outlet malls and short-order restaurants, all decorated with Dolly pictures.

We watched TV until I started to nod off at about nine o'clock. It sure had been an interesting day—but with no swim.

The bed wasn't all that great, but it worked OK 'til about 6 a.m. In the cool morning air I covered about a hundred miles through down-to-earth Tennessee horse country, unlike the horse country up around Lexington, Kentucky that I toured last year. People here aren't prosperous but they are definitely horse people. The houses are old but there are horses grazing near houses, with no expensive-looking fences, on almost every property. Horse country in the morning, like everywhere else in the morning, makes me hungry.

A LADY NAMED ROSE

In the middle of nowhere, on a road near Greeneville, Tennessee, I found Rose's Restaurant just in time. I was fearing that I'd starve to death. No other customers were in the place so I chatted with Rose as she fried up my breakfast. By the time it was ready, we had become friends and as she served me at a table, she brought herself a cup of coffee. After a little more "get acquainted" talk, I observed that since there was no town nearby, I wondered how she could survive, serving bacon, eggs and coffee for just a couple of bucks. She said that since she was only eight miles from Interstate 81 and opened very early, the business from friendly CB-equipped truckers paid the rent. A couple of them came in while she was sitting talking to me about my trip.

"Hey, Rose. How yuh doin'?"

She told me her only significant profit came from Friday and Saturday night people when she had music by a small local band. There was nowhere else to go and she drew country people from about a 30-mile radius. I wished I could have waited around to see them.

As Rose went on asking me a few personal questions about my life and travels, I began to get the idea that she was toying with the idea of breaking out of her lonesome routine. Just as this occurred to me I noticed it was getting darker outside.

Once outside, I realized I had eaten too much breakfast. I looked anxiously at the Tank Bag. That's a leather bag about the size of a breadbox that straps on top of the gas tank. It has a window on top for a map. It's occasionally a bit of a strain to get my right leg over the saddle, between the luggage and that Tank Bag. I have to stand back on my left leg, raise my right leg out straight and hop forward with it over what's left of the seat. Then I hop forward on my left leg. On this day, once on board, I sat there a minute, resting from the mounting ceremony and loosening my belt a notch to let some of the breakfast spread out, while the bike's shock-absorbers considered whether they could tolerate the situation.

Rose left her other customers to get their own coffee for a minute while she came out to suggest I not head out into the threatening storm.

PLAYING CHESS WITH LOKI

The Norse god, Loki, (God of mischief and wickedness) had noticed what I was thinking about suggesting to Rose, so he started assembling dark clouds in the southwest for an attack in my direction. I was considering heading west, across the cloud front, but this seemed to irritate Loki. I saw the clouds set aside some pawns and advanced both their Queen's Bishop and Queen's Knight in my direction as a warning. So when I saw the big blue "to Route 81," I cancelled thoughts about Rose and plans for more Kentucky and West Virginia riding, and reluctantly eased off toward 81. As I threw more logs into the Honda's boiler, I heard a crash of lightning behind me and imagined a voice from above,—something about "Where's your great sense of freedom and independence now, Sonny."

The storm chased me up Interstate 81 to Abingdon, Virginia, hovering over my left side and flashing loud "Check" signals to the ground whenever I thought about leaving the highway and slipping left under the storm to the old Route 11 and West Virginia. By the time the storm and I both got to Natural Bridge, Loki ordered that I be soaked. It was still early, but soaking wet, I could see I was beaten, and got off to the east, to check into a motel near Steele's Tavern. It was raining too hard for me to unpack unload luggage. To make matters worse, my room was located where I could look out the window and see the GoldWing standing in the rain with my entire luggage on her back.

I had given Rose a rosy picture of travel by motorcycle. It was best that she didn't chose to experience Loki's judgment.

SOMETIMES IT GETS LONESOME

Ending a day's ride early because of rain is an unpleasant aspect of motorcycle touring. Unless I make a connection in the motel bar, I get a lonesome feeling sitting in a room, even when I have a good book with me. It's not near as bad as waking up in a tent when outside it's pouring rain; no bathroom, no TV, no breakfast, not even a cup of coffee. Then there is a wet tent to deal with when the rain stops and the best part of the day gone.

Boredom can also be a problem on any long section of highway riding. Route 95 is boring the whole way between Daytona Beach, Florida, and Washington, D.C. (From D.C. on up to N.Y. it's another kind of grind.)

And I hate to admit it, but occasionally I have been cruising with no idea where I can find my kind of small town or campground when a feeling of frustration dampens the very thing I like best about traveling alone—which is not having a plan.

In the morning after my early stop off of 81, the storm was gone, but Loki had left an army of Rooks hovering over the entire then-known world. Weather reports on the morning's Today Show warned storms were likely to come back. So as I dried off the bike seat while thoughts about touring and camping faded into plans to get on home and wait for a better day. So I faced the end of my first tour with my new Honda. But there would be many more.

Strangely, as started toward home, my mind went back to many of the trips ending on the BMW, when I had the secret urge to pat its tank and thank it for a safe and happy trip. Much as I liked the new machine, an unfocussed collage of about 15 years of BMW-related memories flashed on the edges of my mind. Seems like a dumb thing for the mind to spend time on when a man returns from a long trip to the warmth of a lovely wife.

10

CANADA

CROSSING LAKE ERIE

In the last 40 years, crossing the border into Canada has been almost as easy as crossing a state line in the U.S. I've crossed it in about a dozen places between North Dakota and Maine. But the most unusual crossing was on a Ferry-ship from Sandusky, Ohio, to the southernmost point of Ontario.

PELEE ISLAND

Sandusky is the launch point for a ferry that goes across Lake Erie to Ontario. I've taken it a few times because I like to get off when it stops at Pelee Island, a small island about 6 miles by two miles, half way across Lake Erie. I like to motorcycle around this charming-but-bleak old settlement where life seems so much like it was back home in the 1930s.

In the late 1700's the island shipped red cedar and stone to both Canada and America. This ended when they got into making wine in the late 1800's. (Now think about that.)

I like the antique and isolated nature of the place, which is a little like Tangier Island in the Chesapeake, but without the heavy emphasis on fishing. Everybody knows everybody. Some gas pumps there are still like those of my youth, requiring that you hand pump a batch of gas up into a calibrated glass cylinder at their top and check to see if it's nice and clean before releasing it for gravity to feed it into your gas tank. When was the last time you saw one of these?

The shore lines are like those on the Ontario shore of Lake Erie, where the Loyalists had settled during the American Revolution. Residents park their old cars by the Lake Erie shore, take out tiny folding tables and chairs from their car trunks, plug their little water heaters into the cigarette lighters of their cars and sit to have tea and scones with butter and jelly, served on real china, and on small white tablecloths. I've seen a few of them in the sun along the shores of the lake, and once, on Pelee, when stopping to take a picture, I was invited to join an elderly couple for tea. My hasty impressions may be wrong, but the tiny township on the island seems to have been relocated from the north shore to the west shore where the ferries dock with supplies. Both locations have old government-style buildings. I saw no bars, so unless I stayed over at a B&B, I couldn't find a candidate for a leisurely talk. I learned most of what I know about the Loyalists from the couple I had tea with.

THE LOYALISTS

You may remember learning about the Loyalists. They are the people from the American colonies who preferred to remain loyal to the king during the revolution, preferring law and order to the mob rule that was being called democracy (actually republicanism). Thousands of them moved to Nova Scotia and the Ontario section of Quebec rather than participate in the revolution.

They suffered greatly at the hands of the revolutionaries. Their land was taken by their fellow colonists, especially up around Boston, and they were considered traitors by the revolutionaries. Most of the Loyalist families who held out in Boston until Washington's cannons on Dorchester Heights drove the British out, were carried by British ships to Nova Scotia, where they settled in tent villages. Those that lost their lands out in the Massachusetts countryside struggled their way up into Canada and settled in what is now southern Ontario. (I mentioned in Chapter V my stops in Shelburne and Digby, Nova Scotia, where the few thousand of them that the British relocated established a village. They eventually raided the northeastern shores of the U.S. during the revolution.

As I've traveled several times around Ontario, I've been moved by how many of the settlements have British names. The Coat of Arms of Ontario reflects their view: "Loyal she began, Loyal she remains". On one trip I visited London, bypassed Thamesford and Dorchester to tent in a schoolyard in Stratford on Avon, and tent again in a Kitchener campground. To round out my "touch of

Brittan," I stopped for tea in Cambridge and asked if I could join their "UELAC", the United Empire Loyalists Association of Canada. I was turned down because you have to be a descendant of the original group that came from the thirteen colonies. But it pleased some folks in the "Tea Room" that I had asked to join.

ONTARIO'S KIRKFIELD LIFT LOCK

On that trip, from the Loyalist area in Ontario I went Northeast around Lake Simcoe to see the five locks on the way to the fantastic Kirkfield Hydraulic "Lift Lock" at Balsam Lake.

In 1907 this gigantic lock was built to lift or lower commercial barges some 50 feet between the lake heights. To minimize the amount of water needed, clever use is made of two side-by-side gigantic tubs (140 feet by 33 feet. and 7 feet. deep). They are connected so that when a tub full of boats located at the upper lake level is filled, a water valve between the two tubs is opened and the high one's weight pushes water through the valve and into to the lower one, which contains the boat traffic that wants to go to the higher level. It's a "closed system," except that the tub going up stops one foot short of the upper canal's water level. This allows the upper tub to fill one foot higher than the lower tub. So when the valve is opened, the upper tub becomes heavier than the lower, and it—the upper one—drops. You've got to see it to get the impact of moving a dozen boats and barges up and down fifty feet with no machinery involved.

FIDDLEHEADS

On that same trip I enjoyed a special Bed and Breakfast in the town of Picton on Prince Edward Island. (This is the Prince Edward Island in Lake Ontario, just east of Toronto, not the one up north of Nova Scotia.)

I was traveling east from Toronto along the coast of Lake Ontario on 401, the "Macdonald Cartier Freeway," and watching for a town named Trenton. From Trenton there is "Scenic Road" (route 33) that swings out south to cross Prince Edward Island and come back to 401 about 70 miles later. I was headed for a campground along this route in Picton. But on the way I spotted an old "Tourists" sign in front of a very old and very small house right on the shore of Lake Ontario. It didn't actually have a bedroom for guests. I got a single bed in the hall at the head of the stairs and shared the single bathroom with the lady proprietor. (We tried to take turns, but had a few pleasant run-ins.)

We got a thing going-on when the lady helped me hang my wet tent on her clothesline and take a swim off her dock in the Lake. After we got the wet stuff hung and I had the swim, the two of us sat on her tiny back porch and shared a few rounds from my Irish whiskey bottle.

FRYING FIDDLEHEADS

She explained that her husband, who was a construction laborer, commuted the hundred and some miles to Toronto every Monday through Friday with three other local men to compete for work with foreign laborers. There were no jobs available near Picton. To save money, the four men stay in one motel room in the outskirts of Toronto.

Fortified by the Whiskey, and lonely, she seemed to enjoy my stories and I told them all through dinner at a nearby spaghetti place we walked to. I didn't have a cell phone that year, so didn't call Marilyn.

In the morning, after I took another swim, she served me fried "fiddleheads," with fried eggs, fried mushrooms and a fried tomato with fried slices of potato. Also coffee, toast and jelly—but no meat. Too expensive. She gets a fish whenever the neighbors catch an "extra" one before breakfast, but we had no luck that day.

Among the things I learned was that Fiddleheads are a type of fern, shaped like the top neck of a small violin—the part where the string tensions are adjusted. They aren't very tasty, but they are the first green thing that comes up in the spring, which makes them something special to some people. By the time we got my tent and bedroll folded and I left to catch the "Glenora Ferry" to get off Picton Island, I was wishing I could stay around and meet some of the neighbors. Like the folks we talked about in the coal town, (Kopperton) they live in a different world.

I'd like to visit her again some day.

11

ACCIDENTS AND CLOSE CALLS

"'Tis grace hath brought me safe thus far, and grace will lead me home."

—*Amazing Grace*

By now you have to be wondering if I've been blessed by the Norse God, Balder, the one who couldn't be killed (except by a mistletoe bud. Look it up.). "With all this traveling, doesn't this guy ever have an accident?" Well, Balder has kept me from having one worth telling about. But a couple of incidents do come to mind.

THE MAILBOX AND OTHER CRAZY CRASHES

In 1985 a friend from work, Phil Walcoff, (the other "Lucky Electrician" of Chapter Five) asked if he could join me on a trip. He borrowed a friend's motorcycle and after breakfast one morning we loaded our cycles in my garage, kissed half a dozen people goodbye, and started down on our trip. He must have been still waving goodbye when he reached the end of the driveway, forgot to lean into a turn and went straight across the street into a mailbox. In addition to suffering embarrassment, he suffered a broken headlight, a broken turn signal, two broken rearview mirrors and a dented gas tank. We'll come back to Phil later.

On another occasion, Sam had a similar accident. We were zipping over a mountain on a dirt road leaving my folks farm in upstate New York when he didn't lean over quite far enough on a left turn and went crashing into the woods. Here again, no bones got broken and I unpacked my luggage and rode him on my cycle to a medical clinic in Delhi to get his face and arms patched up and some x-rays. We had to get a pickup truck to get his motorcycle and our luggage and return to dad's farm.

A "NEAR" ACCIDENT

A "near" accident happened one cold morning when I was tailgating a fourteen wheeler near Sturbridge, Massachusetts. I had foolishly put notches in two sides of the windshield (known as a "fairing") so that when the handlebars were turned fully to left or right, they would not cause the rear view mirrors mounted on them to hit the fairing, which doesn't turn. The Fairing stays attached to the main frame of the motorcycle. As I was being pulled along by the "suction" close behind the fourteen-wheeler, (NASCAR guys call it "drafting") another large truck traveling in the opposite direction went by us in the left lane. Its "bow wave" of air pressure slammed into the pocket of low pressure I was riding in and the sudden increase of pressure on my windshield caused it to break horizontally across where I had cut the two notches.

CUTOUTS IN WINDSHIELD

The top half of the windshield slammed into my chest, cutting my chin to add a bit of blood to the picture. I wiggled to a stop on the right shoulder of the highway. In shock, I swore at both trucks, the makers of the fairing, the construction guys who built the highway, and the cold weather—before I was willing to acknowledge that notching my fairing was a stupid thing to do.

I rode on without the fairing to Bedford, Massachusetts, where my employer had a machine shop and some sheets of Plexiglas. I cut out a replacement windshield using the bottom half of the broken windshield as a template and assembled the replacement using the mounting hardware that was still it on the broken one.

THE RECAPPED TIRE

The closest I've come to a serious accident was when I hit a recapped-tire tread as I was leaving Kopperston, West Virginia.

I was riding out of Kopperston and thinking about what the elderly lady I had left on her porch had said about "riding all over the country without your wife."

While cruising at about 60 mph in the "suction" space behind a large truck, my eyes drifted into focus on a large piece of rubber recap on the right rear wheel of the truck right in front of me as it began to slap the road. There's a special version of "panic" that motorcyclists experience quite often when something appears in front of them that it looks like they are sure to crash into. It causes the hands and face to sweat, the mouth and throat to dry, the heart to pound and all muscles to stiffen. This kind of panic began to form as I imagined what might happen next.

There was a second truck pressing several yards behind me, so I couldn't hit the brakes, and I was going too fast to swerve onto the shoulder. Neither could I ease left to pass because I couldn't see far enough around the monster to tell what might be coming toward me in the oncoming lane. I still remember taking a vise-grip on my handlebars as the flailing rubber got longer with each revolution of the wheel and panic took over as I prepared to bump wildly over the piece when if it tore loose.

Crazy with indecision, and unable to slow down enough to quickly get some space,—because of the truck behind, I forced myself forward toward the left rear tire of the beast, hoping the rubber detaching from its right rear tire would go by me. My adrenal glands each poured a half cup of juice, with two teaspoons of sugar, into my system. When the recap finally tore loose, it didn't go straight back. It turned kind of sideways as it tore off and I bumped over one end of it as the bulk of it flailed by me. It put no lateral force on the bike to modify my forward momentum, so the bump just caused a frightening "ga-boom" as my two wheels and shock absorbers dealt with it.

I continued trembling until the truck behind me, who had seen the whole episode, gave me space to ease off onto the shoulder. Although the entire experience probably took place in less than a minute, it established a lifelong vision in my memory that can still make me sweat if I dwell on it.

The truck ahead went blissfully on as if it was used to dropping recaps, and the guy in back gave me what I interpreted as a sympathetic pair of horn blasts as he passed me wobbling to a stop on the shoulder.

We'll talk more about recaps later. I know of a car that was hit by one of the damned things and got its headlight and right front fender section caved in. Such a hit would probably kill a motorcyclist.

THE DRESS SUIT SLIDE

The only other "accident" that comes to mind is the one where I slid on gravel when turning into the driveway of the place where I worked. I tore the left leg of my pants and the elbow of my suit coat, got some blood on my shirt, pants and suit coat, and had to return home to change clothes and go back to work—again on the motorcycle—and hoping that not too many of my fellow workers had seen me go down.

EMBARRASSING MOMENTS

There have been some other embarrassing moments that weren't exactly accidents. One was on a road through a small mountain town in New York State where I crossed over to the left side to ask a man for some directions. There was a pool of water along the curb right by where he was standing, looking a bit anxious as I steered toward him. My front wheel sank into the pool halfway to its hub. Evidently there had been a sewer grate there at one time and it was gone. Leaves and trash must have stopped up the drain and caused this pool in the road.

The splash my front wheel made sprinkled the man's trousers with dirty water and he may have been glad that I got totally stuck. It only took a few minutes for a small and unsympathetic crowd to gather and witness this, the most exciting event that the town had ever seen. Some thought it humorous. Some thought it stupid. I thought it very embarrassing and definitely not macho.

Still sitting on the motorcycle, I apologized to the man and stupidly stuttered my request for directions. He seemed more entertained than angry about the splash, and chuckled out something like, "How are you going to get out of there?"

While my audience now began to expand, I asked a young man among them to help me lift the front wheel out of the hole and back the bike out. He said OK before he realized what he was getting into. He soon found out as I tried to dismount on the right side of the machine to avoid drowning on the left side. I think it was the first time I had ever tried to dismount on the right. I made it OK—with both shoes full of water.

Because of the motorcycle's Fairing (a windshield that goes down to cover knees and legs), there is no way to get a grip on the bike's frame forward of the engine…The only thing you can grab onto is the wheel itself. That required me to stand straddled with my right leg on the curb and my left in the pool of water that extended across the hole and into the street. My helper had to do a less magnificent version of the same stance at the back of the bike, getting his feet wet to grab the luggage rack and keep the bike from falling over when we pulled it up and backward—toward him—out of the hole. The two of us had to do a crazy waddle-dance to back the thing out of the pool without me stepping into the hole.

I thanked my friend who now had wet feet on this sunny day—and a few of his friends clapped softly as others just laughed and wished they had it on tape…I'm not sure if it was for him helping a stranger or that they were pleased to see me leave town. I decided not to sue the town for open sewer covers as I idled off without getting my directions…

The only other embarrassing incident that comes to mind occurred in McLean, Virginia. I was sitting at the head of a long line of cars when the light turned green. I shifted into first gear and gave it the gas—but the bike wouldn't budge.

As horns started blowing, I awkwardly rolled the bike across the face of the three lanes of traffic and into a private driveway where I sat and said a short prayer. God scolded me for not recognizing the symptoms. They were like a broken chain on a chain-drive motorcycle. You can put it in gear and race the engine—and the rear wheel doesn't turn. On the shaft drive BMW there is a U-joint connecting the engine's drive shaft to the drive shaft of the rear wheel. A rubber "boot" covers this U-joint to keep it clean. I backed the boot onto one shaft and found in it the four machine screws that connect the two flanges on the U-joint assembly. The bolts had worked loose and the last one dropped into the boot while I was idling at the stop light.

It was easy to put the four bolts back with the famous BMW tool kit. But it took an hour of fretting about the situation, my suit, my dinner, the traffic and the lady whose driveway I was in. It was definitely another "not macho" event.

FEAR OF AN ACCIDENT

On the day I left on this year 2003 trip, I got the full shock—the panic syndrome, of an accident without having one. As I was heading north at about 60 mph, in the rain, on route 17 towards Winchester—and thinking about writing this piece—when my musings were interrupted as I snapped awake to see a car speeding up to a crossroad just twenty feet ahead of me and screeching to a stop with its nose protruding into a piece of my road.

About once on every trip this happens. It seems likely that drivers see my headlight (on) but need an extra couple of seconds to decide whether they should make me fall down for a long emergency slide, or should they avoid the possibility of me crashing into their vehicle—which might make dents in it—as well as in me. Maybe because I'm smaller than a car, their mind says I appear to be further away. Maybe it's easy to misjudge my speed. And they have to think about all this as they roll out in front of me before they decide whether to hit their brakes. Anyway, it seems that the guys who consider breaking into traffic are a lot more cautious about a possible car crash than a motorcycle crash.

In any event, when I'm on a wet road at 60 mph and a car looks like he might enter from a side road or driveway, I have to carefully ease on the brakes and begin to decide on the left lane or right road shoulder. This kind of event keeps me on edge for the following hour.

I was probably still spooked by the incident when about an hour later, up in Pennsylvania, I came toward another "intruder" and, with my heart speeding up as the bike slowed down fast—I found it was just an empty pick-up truck "for sale." It was protruding well into the right lane to make sure that everyone going north on PA 522 would have to pay attention to it.

Glad it was just a false alarm; I tried to absorb the shot of adrenalin with more peaceful thoughts. In this mood, I saw a sad motorcycle parked on the front lawn of a house. I say sad because it looked like it didn't have a friend, leaning deeply to its left (the kickstand side), with its front wheel drooping to its left making its headlight point down. It had a "For Sale" sign wired to its saddle. It seemed like it knew that it was no longer needed.

Speaking of signs for a minute—one of the good things about traveling on back roads is that there are very few commercial signs, the big ones that police hide behind. An occasional "Auto Repair" or an old chewing tobacco ad painted on a barn are the only things available to read. So I spend a lot of time reading yellow "deer crossing" signs. To me they look more like happy deer dancing or prancing on their back legs. You've got to have an imagination if half your ride is taken up reading signs like "Truck Entering", "Tractor Working", "Amish Wagons Ahead", "Cow, Sheep or Horses Crossing", "Children Playing", "Fire Engines Entering", "Moose Area", or "RR Crossing".

FLAT TIRES

One late afternoon Sam and I were on a road in the woods somewhere up in the Adirondacks in a light rain when Sam's cycle started to weave. He got it to a stop in front of the only house we had seen for miles. His rear tire had gone flat.

I wished it had been mine because it's so easy to remove a rear wheel on a shaft drive BMW—and with the BMW tool kit tire irons I've been able to repair a flat on the road without help. But this time it was Sam's Japanese chain drive, a real dog to get a wheel off of. Still it's a one-person job and Sam was more or less useless, so he sheltered himself on the big old-fashioned porch of what turned out to be an empty roadside house, while I got the tire off.

I put the luggage from my cycle on the porch with Sam and his cigarettes, bungee-corded the tire onto my luggage rack and headed down the road in the rain. In retrospect, I should have taken the wheel up on the porch, out of the rain, and used my tire repair kit. But that's the kind of chore it's nice to get out of.

It was somewhere around a half hour to a gas station and there they only pumped gas. No mechanic. They pointed me to another station about a half hour further down the road…Here they wouldn't do the job either because the motorcycle wheel wouldn't fit on the thing they used to break a tire from the wheel's rim. But they did let me use two "somethings" as tire irons (old carjack handles, broken screwdrivers or pinch bars)—and their compressor, to do the job myself. That took me an hour or more after which I had about an hour ride in the rain back to where Sam was. By now it was almost dark. I was in a very bad mood, having discovered that the famous Adirondack Black Flies do not always go to bed at night and that they like to chew on people even when it's raining.

With no streetlights in the mountains, we then had two choices. Leave the repaired tire and wheel and luggage on the porch and both ride on my bike a couple of hours in rain and dark to find shelter, or wait on the porch with the flies until daylight. Sam had snoozed most of the afternoon and had remained dry on the porch, so he was bored. He couldn't complain because I was wet and crabby. Since neither of us could face dealing with my tent in the rain, we decided to stay on the dry porch until morning.

The rain was down to a drizzle and the summer night was reasonably warm. I put on semi-dry skivvies and with my head on my luggage, fell asleep swatting flies while Sam sat and smoked cigarettes to keep them away until first light.

Although it got chilly before morning, the rain had stopped. We put on damp jackets and re-mounted the motorcycle wheel using wet wrenches. The drive chain and all the wet hardware survived in tact. Having missed dinner the previous night, we hurried up the road to find breakfast and a place to wash up somewhere north of the two gas stations I had visited the night before.

So now maybe you can appreciate why, 40 years later, I still think of Sam when I see a guy sitting on a porch when it's raining.

Of course I've had to deal with flat tires quite a few times over the years, but the flats that were on other peoples motorcycles stand out in my mind more than the few I've had on my own machines.

Another of the few times I rode with a companion, it was my daughter's boss. His Ducati got a flat on the Virginia Skyline Drive, miles from nowhere. Unlike Sam, he knew how to remove the wheel and replace it. But I still had to unload my luggage so I could tie his wheel on my bike and make the 50 mile round trip down the mountain to get it repaired in Stuarts Draft, Virginia.

While I was gone, a Trooper fussed that we didn't have the Ducati far enough off the road (due to a steep drop from the shoulder). But he, the trooper, was good enough to park nearby and alert traffic with his car's red light blinking. This time it all happened on a warm and sunny day, so we chalked it up as our "first adventure" since leaving home.

Considering the years and miles and places I've traveled, the number of dogs, deer, moose and other critters (including children) on the rural roads, and the difficulties that automobile drivers have with seeing motorcycles, it's amazing to me (and my family) that I have had no serious accidents.

12

THE END OF A TRIP

Coming home from a trip is usually just as enjoyable as leaving on a trip. Each has its own set of anticipations, anxieties and sense of excitement. But returning home requires giving a bit more structured thinking than a departure does. It starts when the traveler begins to speculate on how he will address the situations he knows something about, a thought process he had abandoned when he departed on the trip.

MUSINGS

In the Introduction, I made a big thing about the pleasures of leaving the routine patterns of one's daily life for a spell away from home. But of course this is not the magic key to a happy life. The truth is that it is what the traveler goes home to after his trip that really determines the quality of his life.

My "return" actually begins when I rather suddenly sense that I've had "enough"—even though at that moment I may still be heading away from where I live. It's not that I want to get back to my regular routines. And it's certainly not for want of communion with fascinating people. It's more of an almost subconscious yearning to be with my loving wife.

Once again there is a metamorphosis. My body chemistry seems to change. Small seeds of excitement and anticipation mix to create a fuzzy version of anxiety, one that has no real focus for the mind to deal with. Saying it another way, there doesn't seem to be any specific association between the anxiousness and exactly what is causing it. Anyway, it's definitely not an unpleasant feeling.

As you may have noticed, I have not mentioned much about scenery. In my efforts to report experiences, I have dwelt more on situations where the motorcyclist experiences things that most other people haven't experienced, or, as in my case, he takes the time to communicate with people and get to know about the history of the places he visits.

The more-or-less static beauty of the countryside is of course a major attraction for anyone who travels and most travelers wish they could "get to know" more about the people and places they see. As you have seen in this book, that has been my focus and pleasure at every place I have been.

I suspect that although dozens of the friends I have made in my travels have said they "would give anything" to be able to travel as I have, that they, like my wife, do not really envy me some of the "uncomfortable" aspects that I may have made light of. Perhaps the most disheartening is having to deal with rain. Cars are far more comfortable. But, as I have pointed out, the motorcycle works magic if making real contact with people is an objective, especially people who have different backgrounds and cultural preferences than those of the traveler. To the best of my knowledge, no other motorcyclist has pointed out this "magic."

And so, when I am at home, rather than trying to explain my focus on people, I tend to minimize what I like best about my travels in favor of descriptions of the beauty of the country and general hospitality of its people. I can't end my story without observing that almost every trip I've made has increased my appreciation of this beauty and the magnificent glory of the American and Canadian countryside. It is a feeling that is hard to transfer to someone else. Very few magazines can picture it anywhere near as perfectly as the motorcycle rider can.

My mind plays with these kinds of thoughts as I ride familiar roads to get home. When I come east through the George Washington National Forest, or cross the Shenandoah Valley and the Allegheny mountains and enter the world of close-together houses, traffic lights, gas stations and shopping malls, this kind of thinking fades away. The (mild) shock effect of the traffic somehow organizes my senses to deal with the traffic decisions, the dynamics of three and four lane traffic and blinking red turn signals. Thinking about my need for "readjustment," my inner child begins to step back and look at me for guidance.

The same man who for the last two weeks couldn't remember which bag his watch was in, and didn't care, now has to be concerned with what time it is, and what time it will be when he arrives home. As he once again begins to organize his thoughts, his mind uncovers a bunch of lists and schedules that he had temporarily forgotten.

And if he keeps remembering things, there's a good chance he will miss that last turn.

EPILOGUE

My interest in motorcycles has developed from an early love of the machines themselves through a love of riding to distant places and on to a deep appreciation for the great variety of experiences that my motorcycles have actually enabled. If I haven't traveled further than other motorcyclists, I believe I have enjoyed personal, one-on-one, interaction with more people than almost anyone I have met or read about in other travel books. And it has been the motorcycles themselves—with my Virginia license plates and camping luggage on board that have been the key to making these friendships. A motorcycle catches almost everyone's eye. The license plates generate curiosity. And each new conversation adds not only to my own range of interest, but also to the interests of the people I meet.

I have now reached a state where almost every conversation reminds me of some aspect of my motorcycle memories—and I find it increasingly difficult to keep them to myself. It's so bad that my wife can usually sense which memory I am dealing with, and can give me an appropriate smile to help me refrain from repeating it.

In September, 2005, after I finished writing this book, my son, John, from Maryland, and my grandson, Chris, who flew in from Chicago, and I, motorcycled together for a week, covering 1400 miles in five states—mostly in the Smoky Mountains.

The beat goes on.

My e-mail address is <u>wfmason@adelphia.net</u>

Index

978-0-595-38622-2
0-595-38622-9

Printed in the United States
62282LVS00004B/214